# GOD'S EVANGEL:

BEING

# GOSPEL PAPERS

BY

*F. W. GRANT.*

WIPF & STOCK · Eugene, Oregon

Wipf and Stock Publishers
199 W 8th Ave, Suite 3
Eugene, OR 97401

God's Evangel
Being Gospel Papers
By Grant, F. W.
Softcover ISBN-13: 978-1-7252-7562-1
Publication date 3/30/2020
Previously published by Loizeaux Brothers, 1926

## CONTENTS.

|  | Page |
|---|---|
| A Coal from the Altar | 3 |
| In the Pharisee's House | 8 |
| At the Well | 19 |
| A Brand from the Burning | 32 |
| Rahab | 48 |
| The Demoniac | 62 |
| The Gospel in the Genealogy | 74 |
| The Healing of the Issue | 88 |
| The Famine of Samaria, and How it was Relieved | 96 |
| The Lost Sheep | 106 |
| The Lost Piece of Silver | 117 |
| The Lost Son | 122 |
| Not Lost and Not Saved—(the Elder Son) | 134 |
| The Perseverance of the Saints | 141 |

# A COAL FROM THE ALTAR.

## A GOSPEL ADDRESS.

(ISAIAH, Chap. vi.)

THE lesson of this chapter, as we in our day may read it, is very full in its evangelic teaching. Its two broad features are these, that, let man but take his true place before God, he shall surely find God's mercy for him; and then, also, that this *mercy* is, and must be, also *righteousness*. As the apostle puts it concerning the gospel: "It is the power of God unto *salvation* to every one that believeth." And then, why? "For therein is the righteousness of God revealed." In God's good news to fallen man is His righteousness revealed.

The prophet, though he be that—God's man toward the people,—in the presence of God must fall as low as any other. A Manasseh or a thief on the cross could do no more than utter that cry, "Woe is me, for I am undone; because I am a man of unclean lips." And that is all the man of God can say. Like the Psalmist, "Enter not into judgment with Thy servant, O Lord! for in thy sight shall *no man living* be justified."

It is the first essential thing for blessing to be brought just to this point, to the utter giving up of all pretension to anything before God,—to the acceptance of His sentence of utter condemnation upon all the world,—all the world guilty before God. When we have reached that point we do not look round with self-complacency upon our neighbors, to reflect upon how much guiltier they are than we. That word "LOST," if we know what it means, swallows up all other distinctions. It refuses to know any distinction. "Undone!" "Lost!" The sinner of the city and Isaiah the prophet absolutely upon the same level as to that!

Have you come down to that dead level, reader? Death is, you know, the abolisher of all distinctions. Men are dead,—*all* dead,—dead in trespasses and sins alike. Oh the hopelessness of that condition! Can you educate or improve death? Can human power do aught with death? No; God alone can quicken. You must have "life." You must be born again. No works can come of you but "*dead* works," nothing that has not the odor of corruption in it, until you are born again, born of God, born of *His word*, which liveth and abideth forever: "and THIS is the word, which by the *gospel* is preached unto you." (1 Pet. i. 25.)

Where and as you are then,— utterly powerless and helpless,— doing nothing, being nothing, promising nothing, you must receive the sweet and gladdening message of God's good news. You can be nothing, do nothing, till you have received it; for you are born again *by* it, and only so. You do not even begin to live to God until it does its work upon you.

And now, mark. No sooner is there the acknowledgment, "Woe is me, for I am undone; because I am a man of unclean lips," than the mercy of God supplies the remedy. "Then flew one of the seraphim unto me, having a live coal in his hand, which he had taken with the tongs from off the altar; and he laid it upon my mouth, and said, Lo, this hath touched thy lips, and thine iniquity is taken away, and thy sin is purged."

How blessed, how worthy of God! No long laborious process of cure is here! No conditions are imposed, no work of self-help is enjoined. The provision of grace is simple, immediate, and immediately effectual, then and there. On the sinner's part is solely the confession of ruin which sin has wrought. The declaration of iniquity taken away and of sin purged meets it at once on God's part. It is preached to the "undone" one. God's word gives him the assurance of what is done for him. He is not left to examine himself and to search out by his own feelings what is the mind of God toward him. He has to believe only, and be at peace.

And so it ever is. Everywhere the gospel proclaims for all, because all are sinners, the good news of a salvation provided just for sinners. The call is to "repent, and believe the gospel,"— that is, to take the place of sinners, and just drink in the mercy provided for sinners. To "repent" is to give up the pretence and effort at *self*-justification. To "believe the gospel" is just to believe in the justification which God has provided.

"Being justified *freely* by His grace." "Freely,"— what does that mean? "Whosoever will, let him take of the water of life freely." What *is* taking it freely? Surely, just believing that it is mine, unconditionally mine, because I want it. That I am to assure myself that it is mine if *I* "will," without any further question. This is the only "appropriation" Scripture knows of. The prophet confesses himself "undone." He is a needy, anxious, convicted one. He is thereupon assured that *his* iniquity is taken away, *his* sin is purged. That is what he is called on to appropriate. Not something that is not his own, but something that is freely his, just upon the ground of his being a poor, lost one, needing it.

Many, if I could ask, Do you need a salvation such as this? would have no difficulty at all in giving answer that they did. And further, if I asked them, *would* they have just such a salvation, if they could, would think it folly to ask such a question. With *them* the question is of God's will, not of theirs. In Scripture the question is of man's will, not of God's. "How often would *I* have gathered thy children together, even as a hen gathereth her chickens under her wings, AND YE would not." "Lord, if Thou wilt, Thou canst make me clean." "*I will;* be thou clean." "Who would have all men to be saved, and to come to the knowledge of the truth." Thus, if *we* will, there is no difficulty. For lost ones God has provided salvation, through the work of Jesus. If *we* are that, and would have that salvation, it is ours. It is not for us to question, but to believe our blessedness.

But what a strange mode of purging unclean lips! "A live coal" from the altar. A coal red-hot with the fire which has just been consuming the victim. Yes, "*our God is a consuming fire.*" What a picture of that indignation and wrath against sin, which is a necessity in the nature of a holy God! And though he pity, yea, love the sinner, *that* cannot change His holiness. Set me in presence, then, of this righteous and holy God, how can He show me favor? How can the *righteousness* of God clear or justify me? It seems as impossible as that a "live coal" should purge instead of blasting human lips.

But look again. It is a coal from off the altar: a *live* coal still, for God's wrath against sin never can die out, God's righteousness never can be aught but what it ever has been. But this live coal from the altar of sacrifice is nevertheless changed in its character so far: it does *not* blast, but purges. And, looking not at the type but at the antitype, the righteousness of God in the cross of Jesus Christ does *not* condemn but justifies the sinner. That cross surely is the altar of sacrifice where the live coal has done its work. It is where the righteousness of God has been declared as nowhere else; but where it is declared, perfect as ever, living and active in its antagonism to sin; and yet not against the sinner, but on his side. So that if I, confessing the sins which prove me one of those for whom He died, take my place thus before Himself, I find Him faithful and just to forgive me my sins, and to cleanse me from all unrighteousness.

God has title to tell out His love,— title to show it *me*, — has earned this title at such cost to Himself that I cannot but believe He must love *much*, and love much to tell it out, and make souls happy in it. The gospel sent out everywhere is His witness that it is so. I cannot honor Him more than by giving credit to it.

Will you, beloved reader, if yet you have not? Will *you* let in this tale of joy which is seeking admittance to your heart at this moment? Is it too good to be believed? Too good for a tale from God Himself? Does it give Him more glory than He deserves? Only take your place with the prophet in this chapter. God's testimony to the work of Christ is this: That it avails for *you;* for you, poor undone one, so glad to have this salvation if you only might, for *you* it avails. "Your iniquity is taken away, and your sin purged." Believe it and rejoice.

# IN THE PHARISEE'S HOUSE.

## A GOSPEL ADDRESS.

(LUKE vii. 36–50.)

WHEN we first wake up to realize that we have not got any real solid peace as to the future,— I do not say hope, for I suppose everybody has something which he likes to call hope, if it is not very solid,—but when we wake up to find no solid ground for the future, we are still, if awake, yet in the darkness. We wake up ignorant how to secure what we are so anxious to secure; and therefore it is that we commonly miss, for a time at any rate, what we are seeking after, because we seek it in a wrong direction. We are very apt to impute it to God, and think God is dealing hardly with us, and that God is not willing to give it to us. We have got to wait upon God we think, until He is ready; whereas God is all the time waiting upon us. We have not to wait at all for God; but we are moving in one direction, and the thing we want to find is in another. Therefore the Gospel has to set this right; putting aside the thoughts and feelings of our own hearts to give us God's thoughts instead. What is meant by repentance? Every one naturally—not merely moralists, but the most ungodly, when he is aroused, thinks it means putting himself right, and thus takes a wrong direction—seeks exactly in an opposite way for the thing, he wants to find. Scripture has to come in and correct our thoughts, to turn us right round upon our path; and then the end we thought we had to go so far to reach is nigh at hand.

We find our Lord here with a Pharisee. These Pharisees were not all hypocrites, though we know there were many hypocrites among them, and the "leaven of the

Pharisees" was indeed hypocrisy. It is inseparable, more or less, from such a position as they were taking, however many who meant to be honest might be taking it. Lawkeepers for righteousness cannot afford to be quite honest. It would spoil their stock in trade if they looked too narrowly at what their hands are manufacturing for God. It is inseparable from their business that they cannot afford to keep a scrupulous conscience; and here they bring in the thought of God's mercy, and hope that God will take their shoddy for good cloth.

The Pharisees, in fact, included almost all the religious people of the day; and they are types of a large mass of the religious people of any day. We can find plenty of them all about us in Christendom now. A class of people who cannot speak of having attained salvation or got peace with God; but whose religious life is a busy industry to provide themselves the wedding garment they must have to appear in before God.

They are not irreligious, and not at rest. They are *sinners* in general, but not *sinners* in particular; not perhaps good enough for heaven, and not quite bad enough for hell; and so, if they do not believe in purgatory, puzzled where to place themselves; but certainly not with publicans and such like. Thus One who sits down with publicans they do not understand. The gospel He comes to announce passes right over their heads and never touches them; or if it touches, it only gives offense.

John the Baptist had come in a totally different way, and in a way more striking, naturally. He had come as a man separating himself from all alike, and altogether. Preaching in the wilderness of Judea, never seen in their cities, never taking part in their religious ceremonies, although of a priestly family, with his strange unfashionable garment of camel's hair, and his food of locusts and wild honey, he stood off from men, calling a whole nation to repentance and to flee from coming wrath.

*He* did not suit the Pharisees either. The "way of righteousness" was not more to their taste than the way of grace. Opposite as he was in so many respects to the Lord, there was one point in which their testimony perfectly coincided. Neither made any difference in favor of religious people. If the Lord received all, welcomed all, the Baptist stood off from all, condemned all. Neither took account of their meritorious striving for goodness. If they went after John they must go with the common crowd of sinners: if one invited the Lord into his house, a sinner would follow Him in even there, as if His presence were sufficient title.

So they believed in neither. When called to mourning they would not weep, and when piped to they would not dance. God's righteousness was too severe; God's grace was too free and bountiful. Bent upon justifying themselves before God, His righteousness condemned them as sinners, and as sinners His grace too alone would justify them. In either way Pharisaism could not exist. Both proclaimed them in a wrong path,— a path in which each step of apparent progress carried them but farther away from the end they sought. All their effort was to establish a difference between themselves and others, while neither righteousness nor grace would make a difference at all.

The strange thing is that we who try in vain to justify ourselves are called instead to *justify God*. For ourselves "it is God that justifieth," and God alone. But we justify *Him* when we take our places according to His estimate of what we are, who has pronounced upon us with a plainness which we cannot (except wilfully) mistake, and an absoluteness which allows of no contention. "The Publicans justified God, being baptized with the baptism of John." They were all baptized in Jordan, the river of death, "confessing their sins,"— the sins of which death was the just due; and thus they proclaimed God's righteousness against themselves. That was repentance; and there it was that God could proclaim *their* righteousness whose testimony was that they had none.

The Pharisee here helps to illustrate these points. He asks the Lord into his house; and the Lord goes. You never find anybody seeking for Him whom He refuses or turns away. If He will not refuse to sit down with Publicans and sinners, he will not refuse a Pharisee's invitation either. And so let me say to anybody here: if there be a heart to welcome Him, fear not that He will not come because your measure of sin is not the due measure of it. The offer of the gospel is world-wide, and God knows perfectly how many and various are the states of soul addressed by it; but they are sinful states, all, with all their variety; and a Saviour of sinners is a Saviour for all. Quite true, that if He comes into Simon's house Simon's heart will not escape the testing of His presence, and it will be soon seen if the reception is real. If it is, His word will be submitted to, in proportion as He Himself is known, and has authority with the soul.

Thus all turns really upon what Christ is to us. Faith in Christ Himself — and that means a welcome given to Him — is the beginning of everything to us. Christ is light. To welcome Him is to get the light into our souls. We cannot be in His company without finding out what we are, and learning the only terms upon which we can be with Him; but those terms are surely submitted to, when we so learn them. All really turns upon this, what Christ Himself is to us.

And this is what we find here. Only that the one who welcomed Him in the Pharisee's house was not the Pharisee. Alas, no; the only one found to appreciate the Son of God from heaven was one marked out comparatively as a *sinner*. "A woman in the city, that was a *sinner*, when she heard that Jesus sat at meat in the Pharisee's house, brought an alabaster box of ointment, and stood at His feet behind him weeping, and began to wash His feet with tears, and did wipe them with the hairs of her head, and kissed His feet, and anointed them with the ointment."

What a wonderful attraction there was in Him for sinners! We may be sure that a Pharisee's house would be just the place of all places she would naturally have kept away from. But if He is there, the place changes its character directly.

His presence even in a Pharisee's house could give boldness to the sinner to be there too.

What a wonderful thing is grace, beloved friends! How it changes all our thoughts, all our relationships with regard to God, as we realize it! Where is the man who, after a long life of service to God, could say, as the fruit of that, "I go to God without any fear"? It is just that very class who call it presumption for them to say that. And it is quite true, it is presumption for anybody on that ground. Who but must tremble to draw near to God? But here is a poor sinner who does not tremble. Here is a sinner who gets boldness, by the very fact of His being there, to come in after Him, uninvited, even into a Pharisee's house! And, moreover, He has not said even a word to her yet, that we know of. She has just discerned what is in Him for such as she is, and lays hold upon Him in her faith without a question.

No syllable, as far as we know, had He ever yet addressed to her. Either she had seen Him, and heard for herself the gracious words that were so constant on His lips,— seen, perhaps, the deeds of love by which the words were evermore confirmed,— or perhaps she had only heard of Him through others. Words repeated, it may be, by unbelieving lips, or the story of what had been to the teller but a gaping wonder, may have sunk into her soul to be the seed there of eternal blessing. Any way, faith in her knew and apprehended Him; and in Him found its need met, found what made Him hers, and made her His eternally.

And there she is now in the Pharisee's house, heedless of everything else in His presence. She feels no other eyes upon her. The presence of others neither daunts nor restrains her. There she is with her tears,— not all of sorrow,— to wash His feet; her hair (her woman's glory) abased — was it abased? — to wipe them; her box of precious ointment to anoint them with. All was (how much!) too little for Him. All her wealth could rise no higher than His feet; but He who had come so far to win man's heart to God, valued and acknowledged the gift of love, owned and justified the giver. "She loved much," from His own lips here, is the first word of this kind that meets us in the gospels.

But the Pharisee does not understand it. "He spake within himself, saying, This man, if he were a prophet, would have known who and what manner of woman this is that toucheth him; for she is a sinner." The Lord shows him that He is a prophet by reading his unspoken thought. "And Jesus, answering, said unto him, Simon,

I have somewhat to say unto thee. And he saith, Master, say on. There was a certain creditor which had two debtors; the one owed five hundred pence, and the other fifty."

There was a difference in the amount of the debts: there was no difference in this respect, that they were both debtors. So says the apostle: "There is no difference, for all have sinned,"— not all equally, he does not say that, but all have sinned. Who has not? Who is not God's debtor? Then mark what a personal interest this gives us in our Lord's next words. Simon, or one of us, might owe his fifty pence only; another his five hundred. But if the first made that difference his plea, what would it show but hardness?

"And when they had nothing to pay,"— *there* is another point in which there is no difference, and yet the greatest possible difference, if you look at it in another way. As to *ability* to pay, there is no difference at all. Not alone His holiness could not allow us to compound, but we on our part could not. All we can do is to draw drafts upon the future,— a bank where we have no credit, and where not one of our drafts is honored. We can promise: that indeed is easy; but which of our performances ever did anything else but increase the debt? And if it did not, for which of them, even as a single item, could we presume we had made God our creditor?

If we will take God's word for it, simple enough it is, not only that "there is none righteous," but "there is none that doeth good." In this sense, therefore, clearly, we have got nothing to pay: still, that is not quite yet the sense of the Lord's words. If it were, since all of us have nothing to pay, *all* would be forgiven, whereas forgiveness is the portion of some, not all, and there is a point at which people have to arrive before they are forgiven.

This is, in fact, the point of which our Lord speaks. It is when the having nothing wherewith to pay becomes a truth in our consciousness,— when we reach the fact of our utter bankruptcy,— when we give up the effort to compound with God, and are obliged to take our places before Him as mere beggars,— sinners quite undone,— that mercy becomes actually ours. "If we confess our sins"— that and nothing more —" He is faithful and just to forgive us our sins, and to cleanse us from all unrighteousness."

This, then, is a word meant for any soul in the consciousness of its ruin to take as applying to itself. If the first part consciously applies to you, beloved friends, the second part does. If it be true of you that you have nothing to pay God with, it is assuredly true that He frankly forgives you. Take the sweet assurance to your heart. Keep it, as you have perfect title. Fear not because it is so much beyond your thought. God's thoughts are not as our thoughts; nor is that unbelieving proverb that a thing is "too good to be true" applicable at all where *He* is in question. The really best thing of Him is ever the truest.

"The Son of man is come to seek and save that which is lost." Hear it, ye lost ones. Let it fill up your hearts with joy and adoration. "When they had nothing to pay, he frankly forgave them both." The amount of the debt made no difference in this respect. The Pharisee and the sinner of the city might alike here be met. There was no difference as to the way or the certainty of forgiveness. The difference that this would make would naturally be of another kind. "Tell me, therefore," says the Lord to Simon, "which of them will love him most?" "I suppose," says Simon, forced into honesty by the appeal, "I suppose, he to whom he forgave most." "Thou hast rightly judged," replies the Lord.

The natural conscience thus judges, and judges rightly, that the greater the debt forgiven, the more the heart of the debtor would be turned in grateful love toward Him who had forgiven him.

Love, then, here — and the Lord teaches us in the application that He is illustrating how love to God is produced in the soul — love is based upon the knowledge of forgiveness. Grace is thus the spring of holiness in us. The gospel not only sets the soul free from fear of wrath and condemnation, but *in* setting it free, binds it to God forever. "O Lord," says the psalmist, "truly I am Thy servant: I am Thy servant, and the son of Thine handmaid: *Thou hast loosed my bonds.*" This is the principle. And the apostle says, "And not only so,"— not only is salvation sure,—"but we also joy in God through our Lord Jesus Christ, by whom we have now received the reconciliation."

Thus the gospel provides for holiness by the freeness of its forgiveness, and (mark it well) by the certainty also of the forgiveness which it proclaims. If the love is founded, as it is clearly taught here, upon the sense of what one has received, then it is absolutely necessary to this that forgiveness should be a certainty, far removed from doubt and question. And this is ever what Scripture supposes as to the Christian. It supposes that he has definite certainty as to that which alone gives him his place, and forms his character as a Christian; and the first thing, of course, is forgiveness.

You may turn round on me, perhaps, and say, "I have not had the Lord's voice speaking to me, as the woman in this story had." But that is your mistake, not mine, beloved friends. In the first place, as to the woman here, when the Lord pronounced her a forgiven one upon this evidence that she loved much, *He had not yet spoken to her.* It is a thing which seems to give such remarkable beauty and simplicity to her faith that it had no direct word to herself to go upon. She had seen His acts and ways of love with others, and she had laid hold upon the grace in it for her own need. His lips only confirm it to her,— vindicate that simplicity of faith in her, and show it was no mistake. But the love the Lord speaks of, the love that was manifesting itself in her actions there, was a love based upon the sense of a forgiveness which she already enjoyed, and which was working its blessed work upon her.

And then again, if the Lord spoke to her, He speaks here, beloved friends, no less to us. "When they had nothing to pay, He frankly forgave them both," is a word as definite as can be for any soul who is consciously in that condition. To all beggared and bankrupt souls, consciously that, the good news is here proclaimed of a forgiveness for them as clear, as free, as definite, as heart can desire. If your soul only says to Him, "Lord, I have nothing to pay," then you shall know the grace of a giving God. Without presumption, without pretension to be anything, without having to look into yourself to find anything, except sin and misery, you may, nay, you are called upon to appropriate to yourself a forgiveness which God has pronounced yours. The Gospel does not expect to find ready-made saints: it *makes* them. It is preached not to saints, but to sinners, and the first thing is to receive it as such,— God's good news, declaring the character of God, bringing His love into your souls to *produce* love again to Him. All commandment-keeping comes as the result of this: "If ye love me, keep my commandments." "Put on, therefore, as the elect of God, holy and *beloved*, bowels of mercies, kindness, humbleness of mind, meekness, long-suffering." All such things are fruits of the Gospel; and therefore the Gospel is first of all to be received, in order to them.

The Lord Himself, not judging here in a direct divine way, but by the evidences, pronounces as to this woman's forgiveness from the tokens of her love, contrasting it with the coldness of the Pharisee's reception: "And he turned to the woman, and said unto Simon, Seest thou this woman? I entered into thy house, thou gavest me no water for my feet; but she has washed my feet with tears, and wiped them with the hairs of her head. Thou gavest me no kiss; but this woman, since the time that I came in, has not ceased to kiss my feet. My head with oil thou didst not anoint; but this woman hath anointed my feet with ointment. Wherefore, I say unto thee, her sins, which are many, are forgiven, *for she loved much:* but to whom little is forgiven, the same loveth little."

Mark how gently the Lord deals there with Simon's conscience. He will not say Simon does not love at all. Himself there his guest, he will give him all possible credit for the invitation. He will leave it to his own soul if he loved so much even as "a little." But the woman, with her sins "many," as He says they are, she shall have from His own mouth the assurance of how little ashamed of her He is, or of the grace in which she has had such just confidence. "And He said unto her, Thy sins are forgiven." Let them cavil as they may, He will confirm it. "Thy faith hath saved thee; go in peace."

And may some who listen to me now, with an equal simplicity, lay hold upon a love whose unexhausted treasury is as full to-day as ever for all demands upon it. May you, too, beloved friends, believing, go on your way rejoicing in a peace made for you by the blood of the Cross, and proclaimed to you by its Maker.

# AT THE WELL.

## A GOSPEL ADDRESS.

(JOHN iv.)

THE Lord had not one stereotyped answer, beloved friends, for those He met. He met souls; He answered souls—not questions even, but souls. And you will find, if you take this chapter for instance, and compare it with the chapter preceding, how differently the Lord answers two cases which were indeed different themselves, but the difference between which would have caused, one might naturally think, precisely opposite answers to those the Lord gave. You find in the third chapter Nicodemus, a ruler of the Jews, a teacher, a man of respectablity, and of religion, one who came to the Lord with a serious inquiry, as a teacher come from God. He owns the divine power which was working through Him; and, while he comes timidly—comes by night—yet by that very act shows himself aware how much he is risking by the coming, how much he is endangering his reputation with the people by coming to the Nazarene. And yet he comes, reverently to own that He is a teacher come from God, and to put himself, teacher as he was, in confessed ignorance, at His feet to be taught.

Now you would think the Lord would have opened at once all His heart to such a man. His first words, you would think, would be words of amplest assurance and unbounded encouragement. Nay; the very first words the Lord has to say are, "You must be born again."

That is not the gospel, beloved friends. Do not ever mistake "you must be born again," for the gospel. It is a very great mistake to suppose the gospel to be any, "you must be." No such thing—you may be assured if it is a "you must be," that it is not the gospel. If a man must be born again, what is he going to do to be born? What does his whole past life count for? Just nothing. What is he going to do for the future? He has got to begin all over again; but how? He has got not merely to live, but to be born. What can a man do in the matter? He has nothing to do with his natural birth. What can he do as to spiritual birth? *He can do nothing.*

It is just a shut door in a man's face, and that is what the Lord intends. But why does He shut the door in Nicodemus' face? I will tell you why. Nicodemus was a man of the Pharisees; one of the teachers of the people who were leading the people all wrong; he was a man who, with all his sincerity, all his honesty, all his desire to be taught—actually did not know, in spite of such Scripture as the Lord referred him to, what was needed to enter into the kingdom at all. He was one of a class which the Lord represents as being able to stand up before God and say honestly enough, in a sense, but self-deceived, "God, I thank Thee that I am not as other men are, extortioners, unjust, adulterers, or even as this publican; I fast twice in the week, I give tithes of all that I possess." Well, was it not true? Why, yes, the Lord never says one word about its not being true—it was all true. Why should he not say it? He does not claim perfection, nor that what he had done was done without God's help. He thanks God for it. "God, I thank Thee, I am not as other men." He was not only a moral man but a religious man. He was painstaking and self-denying, for he gave tithes of all he possessed, and fasted twice a week.

Was not that a most respectable man? earnest, moral, religious. Yet what do you find? The door shut in his face more fully and more decidedly than in that of Nicodemus. "The *publican*, standing afar off, would not lift up so much as his eyes unto heaven, but smote upon his breast, saying, God be merciful to me a sinner." And *he* went down to his house justified. *He* found the door opened; the other man found the door shut. Do you understand and appreciate the difference, beloved friend?

Now here in Nicodemus is just a man of this class, and what he wanted was just what the Lord gave him; for the Lord never made a mistake. Self-righteousness must come to a break down. "You have not begun to live," is what the Lord says to Nicodemus: "you must be born again."

What is one to do? Oh! beloved friends, the very hardest thing for a man is to learn that he can do nothing. But just there is he cast right over upon God.

Now mark, dear friends, I find that truth of the new birth pressed by our Lord, how many times, do you think? Once! On whom did He press it? On a Pharisee! For what? Just to bring him into a state in which he could *receive* the gospel. With all his respectability, and with all his morality, and with all his religion too, he must be born again!

But now, what if you turn to the next chapter? You find a person of an opposite character—entirely opposite —a woman alone, but alone for other reasons evidently than Nicodemus. He by *night* to save his respectability; the woman alone by day—in the midst of the hot day of the East—because people won't have to do with her.

The one is the respectable man, and he does not want to lose his respectability; the other is one with whom if people were found, *they* would lose *their's*.

She comes alone, but not to meet Him. She is not looking for Him. She does not know what she is really coming there for. She comes with her water-pot;—and how often has she done that before. She comes with her eyes, so to speak, fixed upon her water-pot. You would say she is a dead, hard creature. What her life was, we know. How is it the Lord treats her in a precisely opposite way to that in which He treats Nicodemus? How is it that while He shuts the door in the face of the Pharisee, He opens it wide in the face of the sinner? For that very reason. Because she *is* a sinner—for, for sinners Christ died. To sinners God can show mercy. With sinners there is just this one thing: they have not got righteousness to be stripped from them; they have not got reputation to lose; they have not got barriers of this kind to receiving the gospel. What the Lord says explains it all. He says, "the Publicans and harlots go into the kingdom before you" (Pharisees). They go in as a class, why? Just because Christ has died for sinners. God's love is seeking sinners.

A world-wide invitation goes out in consequence of this. Does it shut out anybody? Nobody; but they may be self-excluded. If you had seen over the door-way here to night: "This place is for sinners," would you all have liked to have come in? It is all very well to say, "we are all sinners." But, again, if you had seen over the door-way, "This room is where sinners assemble," would you have liked to come in? That is just the trouble with the gospel. The invitation includes all—Christ died for all. He does not want anybody to be lost. If He came for the righteous He could not have given

## AT THE WELL.

the invitation to everybody. He can now—a world-wide invitation; and oh! beloved friends, man has got to come down to this before God can raise him up; for God's principle is that "he that humbleth himself shall be exalted." We have got to learn our nothingness; we have to take a truthful position before God. He cannot save a man with a lie upon his lips. He can't lift up a man when he is lifting himself up. He will show grace, mercy, love—take up the chief of sinners to show it—but alas! men will shut out themselves by substituting their own terms for God's.

Now Nicodemus wanted to come in on his own terms, but the woman, she, as a sinner, is already where God in Christ can meet her need.

He says, "If thou knewest the gift of God, and who it is that saith unto thee, 'Give me to drink,' thou would'st have asked of Him, and He would have given thee *living* water." Oh! beloved friends, that is the first sweet, blessed assurance to every soul that is on that ground tonight. "If you know the *gift* of God, and who it is that saith to thee, 'give me to drink' thou would'st ask of Him and He would give thee living water." It is quite sure; there is no possibility of denial—He would give you, if you would only take the place of a receiver, making Him a giver; instead of taking the place of a giver, and making Him but a receiver. She does not understand what the living water is. She has the well before her; and she asks, "Art thou greater than our father Jacob, who gave us the well, and drank thereof himself?" There is just a little wonder and reasoning in her heart. "Who is this man, with His strange conduct?"—a little thought,—"How strange of a Jew to step over the requirements of the law, and come this way with His strange thoughts and new talk about 'God's *gift*,' that God wants man to receive!" May not that be a new thing for some of our hearts to-night, to learn that God is indeed more ready to give than you are to receive—to learn, beloved friends, that God has got love in His heart for you when there is no thought or care in your heart for Him? Yet it is true; for the lost sheep does not seek the shepherd, but the shepherd the sheep. He goeth after that which is lost until He finds; and then the joy of heaven is but *His* joy reflected, where all is in fullest sympathy with Him.

And so there is a way in which we can give the Lord to drink. We can satisfy the love that seeks, by just letting it have its way with us, as it desires.

Her heart is touched, her interest is roused; and more —God is before her soul; the light shines for her by which she is to see herself;—because it is only in the presence of God we learn ourselves. Then He goes further; and now mark, beloved friends—she asks Him for water; she says, "Sir, give me this water, that I thirst not, neither come hither to draw." Still she does not know what she is talking about. "That I thirst not" shows that; and the Lord says quietly, in His own blessed, wonderful way, "Go call thy husband, and come hither." He knows all about the secrets of her heart, knows all about what has brought her there a solitary outcast, *knew* all about it when He spoke of that gift of God to her, and how freely He would give, if she would only take the place of receiving, and ask of Him. And He *shows* her that He does—but in such quiet words, just touching the tender spot, and no more, like the physician; as if saying, Is there not something *there?*—not naming it, but suggesting it to her, as if asking, Will you not confide in Me?

When that, alas, meets with no response, He goes a

little further, and shows that He knows about it all; but then in simple words, with no judgment, no upbraiding: He "upbraideth not." *Conscience* might upbraid, and rightly. *His* care is that, in the presence of God and of His love, she might have what would give her truest judgment of herself and at the same time lead her out of herself for healing and deliverance. So unlike our treatment of a sin-sick soul is His! *We* judge people readily enough, and it is easy; but it brings no deliverance. They will neither take it nor thank us for it. *Their* judgment it must be, not ours; and they need other help than this to make it theirs. *He* first of all takes hold of her for God; so that, when the secret of her life comes out, it is the simplest and most natural thing to come to Him as to a friend about it. It is evident He is no enemy. He is not telling it to her as one who is against her. He is against the sin, to be sure, but not against her. Nor, if He is to be believed, is God either. Knowing her life, He has shown Himself for her already. He has invited her, on the part of God, to take a gift that He would surely give. Will she not understand better now those words about that water when she has found that He knows all, and has to own Him as a prophet? She has to own that. "Sir, I perceive that thou art a prophet." She does not run away. She has asked something, she does not know quite what—some great, mysterious gift; and He has assured her she shall get it. She is attracted, held fast to listen to His love, with a dawning sense that He and it are more and other than at first they seemed. He has just shown her a burden that has to be removed, sin that has to be met, if any blessing is to be for her from God; amd she turns to Him with a question by no means idle for her, nor an escape from the tale her conscience told— a question as to how to approach God. "Our fathers worshiped in this mountain, and ye say that in Jerusalem is the place where men ought to worship."

Doubtless questions about forms of worship are often the escape of souls from what is becoming too grave. But this was not the condition of this soul before us now. She had had her life bared to her, had owned Him as a prophet, and worship was to her what to so many it still is—a homage meant to propitiate an offended God. Jacob's way of winning his brother is still a much approved and fashionable way when the question and the Person are of much more importance. "I will appease him with the present that goeth before," he says; "and afterward I will see his face; *peradventure* he will accept me." And with these as with Jacob, acceptance is still a "peradventure." If your religion is of that sort, how can you know when you have done enough? Suppose it should not be just what you estimate it to be in God's sight. Oh, would you hang eternity upon a—peradventure?

Don't take that way! beloved friends. The very uncertainty may show you that you have not got God's way of peace. For "peace" He speaks of. The Lord answers her question in a way that shows He does not deem it a light one or out of the way. The time was coming when worship would not be a matter of going to Jerusalem, or any place at all. Worship, He tells her, has to be in spirit and in truth, in the knowledge of the person worshiped. You must know God. You cannot worship an unknown God really, because worship is a thing of the heart; it is not posture or ceremonial, but the heart poured out in adoration. You must see something in Him to worship. You cannot worship an unknown God. But still, beloved friends, many, alas, worship God in that way, and think He ought really to be pleased with it. After all, they don't know what it is to worship. What is God's name? Do you say "Father"? And if you do, is it mere orthodoxy, or as knowing Him in that relationship? "Worship the Father," He says. Beloved friends, do you go and say "Father" in spirit and in truth? Do you not see that, for this, the question of acceptance must be settled first? Do you feel at home with God? or are you still outside, like that father's son who served his father so many years, and yet music and dancing in his father's house were a strange thing? Beloved friends, are *you* also doing, doing? then, I ask, "Have you got peace with God?" and you have to say, "Well, I do not know what that means."—"What! have you been serving Him so long, and yet not known Him?"

You must worship the Father. "Ye worship ye know not what," saith the Lord. "We know what we worship, *for salvation* is of the Jews." Do you hear that, beloved friends? God is known, the Father is known, by *salvation*. Do you not see, that unless God is known as a Saviour-God, He is not known at all? How do you know Him? As a judge before whom you are going to appear, and then it will turn out whether you are accepted or rejected. That is not salvation. Salvation is His work, not your work. People do not save themselves, they are saved; God is the Saviour, not man. Our blessed God has provided salvation: "Christ is able to save to the uttermost all that come unto God by Him." And the sweetness of that is not merely that salvation is provided—full and real deliverance for man, as there assuredly is—but that salvation is to give you a Father, a real God for your hearts, and in Him a Father to give you ability to worship in spirit and in truth.

Like the prodigal of the Lord's familiar story, turned back to his father's house by famine, for the bread the very hired servants got to the full, when you, in the very midst of your anxiety—at the best, if received, thinking to be a hired servant—find the Father's heart close to yours, and the Father with His arms about your neck, kissing you, (you a sinner, far off yet and in your sins,) God meeting you where you are, because you could not meet Him where He is—you find God for you in the day of grace, God in Christ a Saviour. God, known and enjoyed, is what will make the "spring of living water" rise up in your souls. That is what will satisfy, and abundantly satisfy. You will carry the refreshment with you. Do you want to know where to find it? That meeting-place between God and the sinner—do you want to know where that is, beloved friends? The cross is that meeting-place between God and man. God and man there come together : man in his wretchedness and ruin ; man far off from God ; for why had Christ to go into the place of curse, if man was not there? Why, beloved friends, should the blessed Son of God take that awful place, forsaken of God Himself, if, after all, although sinners, we were of that respectable sort, if not quite good enough to go to heaven, yet not quite bad enough to go to hell? The cross—can you look at it and say, "Christ died for me?" "He died for all," you say. I answer: If He died for 'all,' if He took that place for all, what must their place be? Are you going to make distinctions amongst sinners, who needed such a death as that to bring them to God? Are you going to plead some little difference between yourself and others when, after all, Barabbas' cross was the place for you and them? Sinners, with no title but their sins, no reason that God should meet them but that He delights in love and in mercy—if you are able to take that place that the Lord of glory took, you also may surely say, "He died for me."

Or are you going to take some credit still for something or other in you? Ah, it is not an enemy that is telling you of your sins, but divine love that has come down to you, by the sacrifice it had to make for you, telling you what you are. You are just the sinner who needed such a death as that, and for whom He died. And, beloved friends, that is God's meeting-place for you. If you thus look at the cross to-night, you will see surely how God meets you with a ready-made salvation. "It is a faithful saying, and worthy to be received of all men, that Christ Jesus came into the world to save sinners." If you could add, with the apostle, "of whom I am chief," you would have chief title. Are you sinners? That is all God wants. Take simply, honestly, that place before God; but add nothing to it. Do not say, "respectable sinners," for Christ did not die for such. If you are not quite bad enough for the cross, then you are not such as Christ died for. If you are a sinner simply, take this mercy home to-night. God, in Christ, is appealing to your hearts to receive this love—God is appealing to your hearts as to whether He does not mean well by you when He offers this salvation. And why should you distrust Him? He is keeping back judgment from the world to show you mercy. The Father is seeking. That is what Christ tells the woman: "The Father seeketh such to worship Him." It is not they who seek the Father, but God is seeking men. Beloved friends, will you receive it? Will you give Him credit for it? The Father seeketh such to worship Him.

"I know that Messiah cometh, which is called Christ: when he is come, he will tell us all things."

"I that speak to thee am he," is His ready answer.

And she is met. That seals to her this grace. The cross was not yet; but there was already for her the long-expected one—Messiah, Christ; and He it was beside her by the well, ministering to her, in the full knowledge of her sin, the grace that alone could meet it. This is, for her, God's meeting-place. Christ is in her soul; the living water henceforth will spring up for her satisfaction forever.

Christ is what you want, dear friends. Are you offended when you open the Gospels and find Him in company with sinners? Do you sympathize with the Pharisees when they make this report of Him, that he receiveth sinners? Or will you allow Him to receive these few far-away ones, enshrined and canonized in Scripture, but not the low and ordinary sinners of the present day?

Most welcome news, sweeter than water to those parched with desert thirst! A man that receives sinners, casting out none that come—invites *all* men to Himself, because all are sinners. "Come unto me all ye that labour and are heavy laden and I will give you rest." Whatever your experience, whatever your feelings, or your life. What can a sinner have but bad feelings and *bad* experiences? What is a sinner but a person of bad life?

He had spoken to her by that well, knowing all about her, and He was the Christ—was there, the living proof of what God was. All was there for her; for her who had asked for what she knew not, and got according to His knowlege and His grace.

And now she runs away to tell the men in the city,—the people who knew her well,—that she had found a man who had told her all things that ever she did. You see at once what has fastened itself upon her. If you know the blessed relief of having had all out before God you will understand it. Has he told it to you in that way, beloved friends? So that having no more reserve with Him, you need have no more now with any other? Can you say, with her, "He told me all things that ever I did,

He and I have been together, all my sins out, and nothing but love to me a sinner."

One thing more. If your heart is full, so is His. If He has given *you*, how wonderful to know that you have given *Him!* When the disciples come from the city to which they had gone to buy meat, what do they find? Find Him with his meat and drink already. The shepherd has found His sheep and He does not want the meat to eat. Joy will not let us eat, any more than sorrow, when it reaches a certain height. Such joy is His. Joy to meet one poor sinner by a well, and bring her to rest and to God. And still He is the same—yesterday, to-day and forever the same Jesus.

Only you must be with Him, remember, upon His own terms. You are to be the sinner, He the Saviour. You with your sins and He with His grace. You the receiver, and He the giver. You must be with Him after that fashion, beloved friends, that you may drink in the infinite grace that is in Him, and find not merely salvation, but a God whom your whole soul can bow down before; one with whom you can be at home indeed; one whom you can trust when you can trust nobody whatever besides, and, least of all, yourself.

Beloved friends, that is what God is—God in Christ. Do you want Him to-night? Is there thirst in your soul? Do you want a Christ like that?

# A BRAND FROM THE BURNING.

## A GOSPEL ADDRESS.

(ZECH. iii. 1-4.)

THE words that I have read, beloved friends, apply properly to the receiving back again of the Jews in the last days, when the Lord puts away their iniquity. Joshua the high priest is the representative of Israel, and he represents them both in their iniquity, which God puts away, and in the blessed place into which he is brought afterward. But then God's reception of any sinner, or of any company of sinners, is on precisely the same pattern as that of any other. God has one way of saving, and only one; and therefore we may rightly take, without the least straining, the account that we have of God's justification of His ancient people, the Jews, yet to take place in the last days, to represent the justification of any sinner now.

The doctrine fundamental to the gospel is that there is no difference between man and man;—not no difference as to the amount of sins that anybody may have committed, or the aggravation of them; for, truly, the day of judgment will bring out a difference, and put everybody exactly in his place according to his works, that is, those who are not saved by the gospel. It is true, then, that there are various degrees of sin, and God will judge with perfect equity as to all; but that is no question of salvation. As to that, everybody is precisely upon the same footing: "There is no difference, *for all have sinned* and come short of the glory of God." It does not say, "all have sinned so many times;" but it says, "all have sinned, and *come short of the glory of God.*"

What was showing forth all through the Old Testament times was, that, according to the principle of works no one could ever be admitted into His presence,— no one could see God and live. That is what the apostle refers to: "all have sinned, and come short of the glory of God." God dwelt in the midst of Israel in visible glory. He dwelt in the tabernacle, or in the temple; but, beloved friends, He dwelt there, as you know, in a place that was carefully shut up from men,— out of which men were carefully excluded. Nobody could see His face and live. That was the great truth signified by the veil of the temple. The way into the holiest, the apostle says, "the way into the holiest"— the figure of heaven —"was not yet made manifest." Nobody could go in and see God.

As long as ever the law lasted, that was maintained. If you take Moses on the mount, when the law was given the second time, in Exodus xxxiii., xxxiv., you find that he asks to see God's glory. And God says, "Thou canst not see my face: for there shall no man see me and live"; but He says, "there is a place by me, and thou shalt stand upon a rock: and it shall come to pass, while my glory passeth by, that I will put thee in a cleft of the rock, and will cover thee with my hand, while I pass by: and it shall come to pass when my glory is passed by, that I will take away mine hand, and thou shalt see my *back parts;* but my face shall not be seen."

How much, beloved friends, would you know of a man if you only saw his back parts? What they saw then was God with His back to them, and His face turned away.

That was in the first great day of Israel's glory, so to

speak. Now look at another. When the temple was just reared up, and God came to take possession of it, the glory fills the building. What does it do then? *Drives all the priests out.* And Solomon says, "The Lord said that he would dwell in the thick darkness." (1 Kings viii. 12.) If He dwells in the thick darkness, what can you know about Him? If *you*, dear friends, are thinking of living for God in order to get into His presence, that is God's word for you. All the time the law lasted you saw His back and not His face. He dwelt in the thick darkness. Is there any one of you who depends upon anything of the sort for acceptance, that has ever seen God's face? Is there any one of you that dare say he can stand before Him on this ground? No one can! Because if it depends upon any work of your hands, be it the smallest thing you can imagine, still God is God, and we may work so as to satisfy ourselves very well, but it is another question as to satisfying God. And if I have to satisfy God, beloved friends, I cannot take it for granted that what I do will satisfy Him. I must have His judgment about it, therefore. But this we cannot have till the day of judgment; so we must go on until the day of judgment, and see how it turns out. Alas, and in the mean time you must go on in that awful uncertainty, drifting on, not knowing whither you are going.

I say if there is the smallest thing you have to do to be accepted with God, it will not do for you to say you have done it right. Are you infallible? Has not God said about your heart, "The heart is deceitful above all things, and desperately wicked: who can know it?" And, if you cannot know your own heart, how can you trust its judgment? How can you tell it is not deceiving you?

The fact is, nobody has peace with God on that ground,

and yet there is such a thing as peace. If I go to the
New Testament, I find that "being justified by faith, we
have *peace* with God": and again, "Come unto me, all ye
that labor and are heavy laden, and I will give you *rest.*"
Beloved friends, He means what He says. Is anxiety
rest? Is doubt rest? Is *not* knowing where you will be
in eternity rest? Is it peace to say "I do not think anybody can know whether he is saved"? There may be
indifference and carelessness in all that, but not rest or
peace. But there is such a thing as peace, and *knowing.*
"These things I have written unto you, that ye may know
that ye have eternal life." People say, But that is presumption. Is it presumption to know what the apostle
wrote that we might know? Is it presumption to take
God's word and believe it? The fact is, if you have got
eternity before you, how can you rest for a moment while
the question where you are to be is unsettled? No,
you cannot: it is impossible.

If we cannot meet God upon the throne and in judgment,—if we cannot by all that we can do get into His
presence,—what are we to do? Beloved, *He* has rent the
veil and come out to us. He has come out Himself when
we could not go in. And, Christ's blessed work being
accomplished, He has opened heaven itself to us. Opened
the way of access, by the blood which has been shed for
us; and His free and gracious invitation now from the
heights of glory into which He has gone is still "Come
unto me, all ye that labor and are heavy laden, and I will
give you rest."

Now look at what we have *here*, in this third of
Zechariah. It is a sinner in his sins in the presence of
God. Now, beloved friends, is not that the very thing
you would be afraid to be? What do you think it must
be for a sinner in his sins to be in the presence of God?

When a soul is awakened, is not the first effort, the natural effort, to turn over a new leaf, forsake one's sins, and so get into the presence of God without them? You never can. Whenever you meet God for the first time, you will find yourself in your sins in His presence. Nobody ever met Him in any other way.

God picked out the best man on the earth, and that was Job. The Lord said, "Hast thou considered my servant Job, that there is none like him in the earth, a perfect and an upright man." There was not one like him, and God says it; but when Job finds himself in the presence of God what does he say? "I abhor myself, and repent in dust and ashes." The prophet Isaiah found himself in the presence of God, and probably he might have been the best man in Israel in his day; and he saw the Lord sitting upon a throne high and lifted up, and His train filled the temple. Above it stood the seraphim; each had six wings; with twain he covered his face, with twain he covered his feet, and with twain he did fly. And one cried unto another, and said, "Holy, holy, holy is the Lord of Hosts," &c. And what does Isaiah say? "Then said I, woe is me, for *I am undone;* because I am a man of unclean lips, and I dwell in the midst of a people of unclean lips; *for mine eyes have seen the king*, the Lord of Hosts."

You are not in bad company when you are in company with Job and Isaiah; but what they found when they got into the presence of God was that they were undone sinners. Beloved friends, God alone can remove your sins, and you must be with Him to have them removed; and if you get into the presence of God in the day of His grace you will find Him *for* you. If you get into His presence in the day of judgment you will find Him against you. In the day of judgment He will be a just *judge;*

in the day of grace He is a just *Saviour*. To be in His presence as a sinner *now* is SALVATION.

Job found it so: it was the end of his difficulty. "I abhor myself, and repent in dust and ashes," lifted him right out of where he was, and gave him more than he had before. That confession of Isaiah, "Woe is me, for I am undone, because I am a man of unclean lips," brought the live coal in the seraph's hand to cleanse his lips: "Lo, this has touched thy lips; and thine inquity is taken away, and thy sin purged." And here, again, we get a sinner with his sins, with a stopped mouth in the presence of God, and it is only to find God *for* him and not against him.

God is for us: that is the wonderful reality which the gospel gives. "I am not ashamed of the gospel of Christ." Why? "Because it is the power of God unto salvation to every one that believeth." How is this? "Because therein"—in the gospel, the good news to sinners—"is the righteousness of God revealed." God's righteousness is revealed, *not* in shutting sinners out of His presence, but in GOOD NEWS,— what God Himself can call "good news,"— divinely suited to comfort the heart. If you receive them to-night, you will go away with your hearts as glad as they can be.

God is light. He is love: but He is light. "That which doth make manifest is light." When is a man in the presence of God? When he is revealed to himself, so that he knows his own condition; and, beloved friends, the one thing that he knows as his condition always, when he first gets into the presence of God, is that he is clothed in filthy garments. He is a sinner in his sins, and nothing else.

It is a very easy thing, of course, for people to say "we are all sinners." If that is being in the presence of God, why we are all in the presence of God, for everybody will own he is a sinner. And that Pharisee, when the woman of the city came into his house, I suppose *he* would have owned that, yet he says, "This man, if he were a prophet, would have known who and what manner of woman this is that toucheth him: for SHE is a *sinner.*" Beloved friends, do you know what it is to distinguish yourselves from other sinners, and put the difference to your own credit? No man in the presence of God can feel like that. When a man is in the presence of God he is a real sinner,— a brand for the burning, if even plucked out. That is what the angel of the Lord says of Joshua: "Is not this a brand plucked out of the fire?" A brand plucked out of the fire is a thing put *into* the fire, to be burned. You may change your mind and take it out of the fire, but that is where it was, and it was sentenced to be burned. There is none righteous, says the law itself,— the very law that people appeal to. They say, Did not God give us the law? Well, what says the law? "There is none righteous: no, not one." This is God's judicial sentence. And what is that said for? It is said, beloved friends, "that every mouth may be stopped, and all the world become guilty before God."

Did you ever take your place, with your mouth stopped, guilty before God? Do you not see that is being in His presence? If you are in the presence of God you are only there with your mouth stopped. Not a word about other sinners. Not a word about difference between sinners. Not a word about degrees of sins. And let me say, too, not a word about good resolutions, or anything to the credit side against your sins! A man comes to me and says, "Well, yes, I did so and so; but—" Now, I say "You are going to make excuses." If you say "I have done so and so,"—it is all right. If you add "but," it won't do. You are going to balance your sins with your good resolutions,—going to ask God to look at what you are going to be, instead of what you are. That is not being in the presence of God. Every one who is before God is there GUILTY.

God has given that verdict that every mouth may be stopped. Then, beloved friends, you are not under probation. The trial is over; the sentence has been pronounced; and all your talking is only trying in vain to get God to give you a new trial.

He has pronounced definitely and positively against the whole world. Beloved friends, have you accepted His sentence? That is your only hope. No plea,— no telling God you will do something. If you get into the presence of God, it will be to say "I abhor myself." You do not abhor a man who is going to turn round and be respectable. When you get a man with whom you can do nothing,— an abandoned creature,— you give him up. That is the sort of man you abhor. When I abhor *myself*, I give myself up. I say it is no good trying to make anything of myself. Sentence is passed upon me; and if God does not show mercy, all is over; no looking forward to a day of judgment to be told how it will turn out then. Judgment has come. Judgment has been pronounced. Everybody has not yet got the exact measure of what he will get: that is true; but judgment is pronounced, and all the world is pronounced guilty before God.

"Clothed with filthy garments." Did you ever notice there a remarkable contrast? When it is a question of men's righteousness, you will find the prophets saying "all our righteousnesses"—(that is not our sins,— our *righteousnesses* are not our sins,— our righteousnesses are our efforts to do something,— our righteousnesses are our best performances)—"all our *righteousnesses* are as filthy *rags.*" Not garments; they are not garments at all,— *rags*, "*filthy rags.*" But when it is a question of our sins, God says, "clothed in filthy *garments.*" They are not filthy rags, they are filthy garments,— he is covered with them. His filthy garments are his iniquity. Our righteousness does not cover us, but our sins do. "From the crown of the head to the sole of the foot there is no soundness, but wounds and bruises and putrefying sores." This is man's condition before God. If, now, as God's word speaks to you, you learn what you are, and take your place in that way as a lost sinner,— a sinner covered with sins,— you now know what repentance is. "I abhor myself, and repent in dust and ashes." Not "I abhor my sins." A good many do that: it is "abhor *myself.*" Have you ever said "I am undone"? That is what Isaiah said. He did not say "I am *going to be* undone, if I do not turn over a new leaf." Did you ever say "I AM undone"? Did you ever know what it was to be "*lost*"?

The Lord Jesus Christ came to save that which was "lost." He speaks of Himself as going after the "lost." There is not a soul among these lost ones that is not found,— that the arms of everlasting mercy do not finally inclose. "He goes after that which is lost, until he finds it." The "sinner that repenteth" is "the sheep that is lost."

There is not a word from the sinner in our chapter; not a word from Joshua here. He does not do or say a thing. There he is, a sinner in his sins, wholly dependent upon the mercy and love of God,— upon that and nothing else,— a sinner in his sins, in the presence of God.

What will God do with a sinner in his sins? What can God do with a man clothed in filthy garments? Beloved friends, what will He do with you, if you are there?

Mark,— oh, mark it well!— you have to stand before God in that very fashion, if you have not yet done so. You may defer it; you may put it off; you may refuse to think about it now; you may refuse to take God's sentence home; you may say "Oh, well, I shall have plenty of company, if I am lost. There will be a good many more lost with me." That will not help you when you stand before God. You will find yourself an individual soul,— alone, and not in company,—or, I might say, only in company with Him whose eye will read you through and through and expose you to yourself, naked and deformed, and in your own proper condition. There will be no talking about your company then. There will be no thought about your neighbor. You will be a solitary sinner before God, with only His eye upon you. If you stand before Him thus now, you will find there is mercy for you If you stand before Him then, you will find it everlasting destruction. This is the acceptable time; behold, now is the day of salvation. Now! — *now*, dear friends. And how long is that "now"? Every pulse-beat, every tick of the clock, is a "now." You don't know how many of them are left you. Friends, there is salvation for you to take hold of as instantaneously as that, because God knows what your need is. There is a rope out for souls that are drowning, that they may clutch on the instant. That is what you want. It is all very well for men who don't know what eternity is to talk about having time. If I had a salvation to offer you that required a week to work out, I could not insure you a week. Blessed be God, I have got a salvation *now* for you.

A sinner in his sins in the presence of God! What will God do? Can you trust Him for that? Do you think there is any good thing in God's heart toward you? Do you connect Him with a doctor and a dying bed?—or with the thunder-storm?

Is there any good in God's heart toward man? Do you believe it? *Do* you believe it, beloved friends? We are in a land in which the mass of people profess to believe it. God gave His Son, but they won't believe in Him. If they believed in God they would not think of Him always as a Judge, and in connection with a storm or a pestilence.

Did God give His Son to punish man? Did Christ die to reveal God as a judge? Why was it, then? Is there any good in God's heart toward man? Beloved friends, when you come to this, that there is none in your heart toward Him, then you will be ready to admit that there is some in His heart for you. These two things go together.

Now the sinner has not a word to say for himself. "And the *Lord said* unto Satan, the Lord rebuke thee, O Satan, even the Lord that hath chosen Jerusalem rebuke thee: is not this a brand plucked out of the fire?" May I not do as I like? says the Lord. And the sinner being silenced, the adversary is silenced too. If the sinner has nothing to say, the adversary, too, has nothing to say. If you want to stop the adversary's mouth, dear friends, stop your own mouth, and let God answer for you.

Well, now, it is as simple as possible. "Now Joshua was clothed with filthy garments, and stood before the angel; and he answered and spake unto those that stood before him, saying, Take away the filthy garments from him." That is the way sin is taken away,— just one word from God, "Take away the filthy garments from him." Beloved friends, is there anybody that would like to hear a voice like that to-night? *God has written it there, that every soul that likes may hear it.* Did God write that for *that* sinner's sake? Has He written the blessed words with which He met sinners of old, for their sakes?

No; but for ours. He is the selfsame God to-day. He never changes. He never has any exceptions. Never! He is the same God everywhere, in every case the same, thoroughly trustworthy, never changing. And if you are in His presence now, in your sins, He says, "Take away his filthy garments from him." Do you believe that? Well, He gives you His word. If you do not believe that, He will give you His oath. "He is faithful and just to forgive us our sins and to cleanse us from all unrighteousness." He is faithful, faithful, faithful. Do you know what "faithful" is? True to a pledged word. Faithfulness is in fulfilling a pledge. Somebody has a claim upon me in some way. I am faithful to my word, faithful to what I have promised. "If we confess our sins, He is faithful and just to forgive us our sins and to cleanse us from all unrighteousness." Do you claim that faithfulness of God? If you bring nothing but sins to Him, you can claim it.

There is a confessed sinner in the presence of God. God is faithful and just to forgive him his sins. Has not God pledged Himself? Would He be faithful if He did not keep His word? You ask, perhaps, How can He forgive us our sins after that fashion? Beloved friends, because Christ died for sinners.

People argue, indeed, Christ died for sinners, and therefore you must do all you can to be a Christian, and so to be saved. You take yourselves out of God's loving hands of mercy, which are longing to take hold of you: that is all. You make Him act in righteousness against you instead of in righteousness for you. God does not save in that way. God does not justify people as Christians, church members, and all that. He "justifies the *ungodly*,"—the people who do NOT work for it. "To him that worketh not,"—"worketh not," do you understand? That is God's word, not mine, "To him that WORKETH NOT, but believeth on Him that justifieth the UNGODLY, his faith is counted for righteousness."

Do you think God means what He says? Do you think God does what He says? God "justifies the ungodly." Do you believe that? "Oh, yes," people say, "we believe that." Well, what are you going to do? "*Going to do the best we can.*" Is not that it?—the best we can! Have we to do the best we can to be ungodly? If God justifies the ungodly, must not you be the sort of person that God justifies? Must you do some good to be ungodly? Ah, if you look at yourselves aright, you will find you are ungodly enough already,—ungodly enough to be justified. If you believe that, what do you do? Nothing!—*because* you believe. If you want to do something, you do *not* believe He justifies the ungodly. If you do believe He justifies the ungodly, you do nothing. Christ died for *sinners*, nobody else. He did not die for good sinners, or for the better class of sinners. He found one man who was the very chief of sinners, and He could not leave him unsaved. He took up that man, the chief of sinners as he was. He could not let him go. Because, if He let the chief of sinners go unsaved, people might have said, there is a limit to the power of the blood of Christ. There was one man, at any rate, that the blood of Christ was not sufficient to save. So God took up the chief of sinners and made an apostle of him. He wanted him to speak in men's ears and hearts: "There! that is the sort of sinners I am saving. Those are the sort of sins that the blood of Christ washes off." Come, now, and put in your claim as a sinner to the precious blood of Christ, and you will get remission of sins. God will say, as to you, Take away his filthy garments from him.

But note: He does not simply turn to others to say

that. He turns to the sinner himself. He wants the sinner to know it. He does not wait until he gets to glory to say it to him. He says, "I have caused thine iniquity to pass from thee." He says "iniquity" here in the plainest terms He can. He does not say "filthy rags." He speaks it right out. He wants the sinner to know it.

Is there anybody here who can say, Oh that I could hear such a word to-night! If you are in company with Joshua now, those words will apply to you as well as him. Christ's death can cover you; God's mercy is for you. Still He says, "Come unto me, all ye that labor and are heavy laden, and I will give you rest." Are you such? Perhaps, with doubt and perplexity, and all that sort of thing. Well, will you come? No right or wrong way of coming, if to Him. But, will you come? "I will give you rest." "I WILL give you rest." No uncertainty about it; not "perhaps," not "probably," I will give you rest, but I WILL give you rest. No doubt or uncertainty about Christ; He is the "yea and amen." "I *will* give you rest." He has made Himself responsible about it. Will you put that responsibility upon Him to-night? You cannot help answering as to whether you will come or not. You have answered it already to Him. You may reverse your decision; but you have either said "I do," or "I do not, want it." It is as simple as can be, beloved friends. Nobody can come right, in one way; nobody can come wrong, in another. That is, you know, a sinner cannot come in a right state, with right thoughts and feelings. He comes a sinner; but he comes right if he comes to Christ; for whosoever comes to Him He will in no wise cast out. Christ says, "Come unto me;" but He does not say in any particular way. Oh, beloved friends, if your hearts answer to Him now, He says, "I will give you rest." Just take your place with Joshua; confess your sins—nothing else; and He is faithful and just to forgive you your sins and cleanse you from all unrighteousness.

But He does not merely cleanse you from your sins. "I will clothe thee with change of raiment." What does He do? He puts a robe of righteousness upon you. How is that? He puts Christ on you. Christ has not only died for men, He has gone up into the presence of God for men, and the very highest seat in glory is occupied by that One who was upon the cross for sinners. God has taken the Man who filled the cross to fill the throne of glory; God has taken Him up there in His presence, beloved friends; and there He is, a *Man*, a man forever. He has not merely gone back God, as He came: He has gone back *Man*, and to be a man forever. There is a Man in the presence of God, in the nearest place to God He can be; a Man who has got a place for man, who never needed to get a place for Himself. He has worked for a place for man, and He has got it; and Christ is made of God unto us " wisdom and righteousness and sanctification and redemption." Christ is our righteousness—the change of raiment for the filthy garments of iniquity; and Christ is righteousness to everyone who believes on Him.

Beloved friends, the soul that believes in Christ is as Christ is before God. What Christ is, he is: as righteous, unchangeably righteous; "righteous as *He* is righteous." We are accepted in the Beloved, before God as He is, with all His perfection; with all that God sees in Him for us, and the value of His work is ours with God.

That is the "change of raiment." One moment a sinner in your sins before God, and another moment clothed with Christ before Him, as Christ is before His eyes. And mark, *God* does all that. He does not say to the

## A BRAND FROM THE BURNING.

sinner, take off your filthy garments and put on these. He says to those who stand by, "Take away the filthy garments from him." He does not say put on these new garments. He says, "*I* will clothe you with change of raiment." God does all.

Now what does He say to you? He is faithful and just to forgive you your sins, and to make over Christ to you as your acceptance before Him. Is not God's righteousness on your side now? What do you say? " I am not ashamed of the gospel of Christ; for it is the power of God unto salvation to every one that believeth." Why? "For therein is the righteousness of God revealed." For God must not only be a good God, a loving God, but a righteous God, and His righteousness is revealed. Where? *In the cross.* And is that *against* sinners? No! God's righteousness is revealed in the cross; and that is not against sinners, but for sinners. The cross is death; the cross is judgment. The cross, beloved friends, is not the fruit of good works, or anything of that sort: it is the fruit of sin, although the sinless One took it. And if you want a title to the cross, your sins are the title. Take your sins; put them down in the presence of God; and God is faithful and just to forgive you your sins. Aye, and to give you the whole value of the work of Christ as you prove yourself thus to be one of those for whom Christ died. He will put you in absolute perfection before God, the absolute and unchangeable perfection of Christ forever and ever.

D

# RAHAB.

## A GOSPEL ADDRESS.

(Joshua, chaps. ii. and vi.)

WE have here, beloved friends, a beautiful picture of a sinner saved by grace. Jericho is a type of the world. We know that the things that happened to Israel, as the apostle tells us, "happened unto them for types, and are written for our admonition upon whom the ends of the world have come." (1 Cor. x. 11.) Jericho is a type of the world under doom from God—doom which is continually threatened by His word, which comes only after a day of grace, and a long announcement of judgment. On the one hand God makes and uses this announcement of judgment to alarm souls and wake them up to fly for safety to the hope set before them; on the other hand, because it goes on for a long time, men harden themselves against it, to worse destruction.

Jericho is a striking type of the world under the curse, as we see here, devoted by God to utter destruction (as we know the world is), seated, however fair its surroundings, by the "river of death," Jordan, very near to the Salt Sea, the sea of judgment, into which it flows. The word Jericho means "Sweet Savor," in striking contrast with what it was to God. The whole land really *stank* before God. And this city of Jericho was branded with His special curse.

But this name (which they, of course, themselves had given it) only shows how differently men estimate the **world** from the way God estimates it. How highly esteemed among men is that which is an abomination in the sight of God. Our natural thoughts are totally opposed to God's thoughts.

Most surely, if we look around upon the world about us, we shall find everywhere the tokens of God's goodness. His mercy makes the "sun to rise on the evil and on the good, and sends His rain on the just and on the unjust." That is quite true. And if people call the world fair and beautiful, we can allow fully that the evidences of His goodness, who created it, are not effaced even by the fall, and that assuredly His mercy lingers over it. But if we look at it in its *moral* character, what is it? "All that is of the world, the lust of the flesh, the lust of the eye, and the pride of life, is not of the Father." There is not a good that has not been abused to evil, not a pleasant note which has not been perverted into discord.

There are, of course, plenty of natural resources—things which show us that God had given man a goodly portion naturally. This we believe: and people are finding out these resources, and getting the mastery of them more and more: all that is permitted to man; but there is nothing for God, or for one who sees with God, to rejoice in all that. Do you think there is joy in heaven when people invent railways or telegraphs? Can you possibly suppose that anything of the kind can give joy really up there? You know it does not hinder the display of the greatest wickedness. You know that, on the contrary, people are turning this into ruinous self-confidence—are arguing that, having done so much, they can do more. They have mastered so many difficulties, they will master their whole condition, if you only give them time.

Yet they die! None the less rapidly does the river of death flow down to the lake of judgment. Nothing that men have done or can do has contributed in one iota to remove the stamp of God's wrath, or the sin, which is, alas! everywhere; and if His judgment tarries, it is not hindered by the marvelous development of human intellect, but by His long-suffering, and because that long-suffering is for salvation.

"Jordan overfloweth all his banks all the time of harvest," and that was the time when judgment was, in the Israelitish army, advancing toward the city. The time of judgment was the time of harvest, the very time the citizens were going out to reap their fields, and bring in the products of their labor. Has not that got a voice? Does it not speak? Man thinks God is waiting for His harvest. In one sense He is. Waiting, on the one hand, in mercy, until the last limit of it has been reached; on the other, waiting until sin, too, has reached its full maturity. And then? Why, as they of Jericho never treasured up the produce of their fields, but the swift executioners of God's wrath were the reapers, so, when the world's harvest comes, God, and not man, will put in the sickle.

Alas, because sentence against an evil work is not speedily executed, therefore the heart of the sons of men is thoroughly set in them to do evil. How long a respite Jericho had! Four hundred years before this, the iniquity of the Amorites had already approached the full. (Gen. xv. 16.) Forty years ago God had cleft the waters of the Red Sea, and brought His people through. Their journey through the wilderness, also, was one constant, miraculous display of Divine power. They had only a little while before seen the destruction of those kings of the Amorites, Sihon and Og. They might have known, their hearts were witness, *who* it was that was really coming with those Israelites. It was not their own power which was so terrible, that was plain; but there was One coming with them who had power to dry up seas, and make mountains fall down at His presence.

What was all this but a warning of judgment, which would be gladly stopped by man's repentance? And so it ever is; so it is now. Why give such wide and public assurance that He is going to execute judgment, but for them to take the sentence home to themselves, and so to prevent the need of actual execution? He speaks it aloud; He utters it in men's ears, in order that they may turn to Him. Never a soul turned to Him with a sense of coming judgment that did not find from Him mercy— the freest and the fullest possible. We find a striking instance of this in the case of Rahab here. She certainly had a history with nothing to recommend her in it. Certainly, in all Jericho, there was none who might seem to have less claim to mercy than she: a sinner amongst sinners she plainly was. Yet the one thing distinguishing her from the rest was, that while, with the rest, that delay of judgment only hardened their hearts, she kept it in her heart, and sought escape from it.

There is nothing in that to make anything of her indeed—nothing morally great or meritorious in the desire to have salvation; but yet very great indeed was the result. Just as with the prodigal son, away in a far-off land, there was nothing particularly to recommend him in the fact that, starving and destitute, his hunger forced him to think of the bread in his father's house. Yet in result it set his feet upon the way back to his father. It is nothing to recommend us when, by need and famine, we are forced to turn to God. No! Yet, blessed be His name! we do not need recommendation. That is what we have here. One soul hears in the voice of judgment an invitation, so to speak, to escape from judgment; and that one soul is saved by *faith*. The visit of the spies to the city was made the occasion, in God's hands, of her getting the thing she was seeking. She was part and parcel of the city, shut up in it, with judgment approaching, and except those spies had found their way into the city, there was, humanly speaking, no way of escape for her. God sought and found her there. He never fails to hear the first breathing of a soul after Him. Rahab might have thought herself outside of all interest to the God of Israel—that He scarce would even hear her prayer—yet He had. We make a great mistake if we think the first sighings of a soul in distress are not heard. He himself is in them; and He cannot fail to respond to the cry which *He* has aroused. So here, Rahab, who had nothing else to distinguish her, pronounces judgment upon herself beforehand, and escapes in the mercy of the One coming near to judge. The two spies come to her house, and are the means, so to speak, of dividing between the living and the dead. Theirs was a message of judgment rather than of mercy—they were sent to search out the land; but nevertheless, they are made the means of distinguishing between the city and those appointed to salvation out of it.

Instead of the king and citizens of Jericho availing themselves of any hope of escape from the judgment so near, they only conspired against the men who came. All their thought was to rid themselves of them, and to stop the voice which might have been raised, as in Rahab's case, in their behalf. And, beloved friends, how many are doing this very thing! How many rise up against the message of judgment, as if to stop *that* would be to stop the judgment itself! The judgment comes none the less surely, if it comes silently and unannounced. Yet how many stifle the voice of conscience, and then suppose that judgment is canceled too! But that is plainly as false as can be. Conscience is not the arbiter in any wise. Conscience can be bribed, and falsified, and hardened, almost to any extent. It is God's word alone that gives true witness, whether to His wrath or to His grace. Jericho might be walled up to heaven, and with store sufficient to defy starvation, and her citizens might frame strong arguments from these. But if Israel had no battering rams for the siege, it availed nothing when at God's word these walls fell to the ground. And whatever our hearts may say, though we may be as comfortable as possible in unbelief, it does not make the wheels of judgment linger for a moment. Do we not already see it taking effect on every side? Is not the world as a condemned cell, and each tick of the clock the summons of souls to meet their God? Why must we die? It is God's original sentence because of sin. Ought we not to hear that voice? Does it not appeal to us solemnly on every side, in the stilled and silent voices of our nearest and dearest? People may call it natural; but we do not feel that it is natural. Our hearts bear contrary witness to such words. We feel that if God break the staff of our lives, it is to prostrate us at His feet with whom mercy yet rejoices against judgment,—who can make judgment itself the handmaid of mercy.

A free gospel can be published freely in a world like this to everybody, without exception, and without mistake, because we can be sure that without exception all are sinners. Rahab had no such gospel indeed, but faith in her, with an instinct that belongs to it, laid hold upon God for mercy. The spies—enemies of her people, nature said—were for her identified with the God she sought. She shelters them at her own risk, sends them forth in peace, and commits to them the matter of her deliverance from the doom approaching. She finds them ready to pledge themselves in her behalf, and to give her a token in assurance of mercy. "Our life for yours," they say to her, "we will be blameless of this thine oath which thou hast made us to swear. Behold, when we come into the land, thou shalt bind this line of scarlet thread in the window which thou didst let us down by; and thou shalt bring thy father, and thy mother, and thy brethren, and all thy father's household, home unto thee. And it shall be that whosoever shall go out of the doors of thy house into the street, his blood shall be upon his head, and we will be guiltless; and whosoever shall be with thee in the house, his blood shall be upon our head, if any hand be upon him."

How sweet this assured and abundant mercy! How precious to find these Israelitish messengers able at once to give the needed assurance, without hesitation or peradventure at all! Such is God throughout all dispensations, that those who know Him can always answer for His gracious response to the cry of need. Faith has indeed in her to be in exercise all through; and so it is with all of us. But if she can trust the token they have given her—if she has confidence in those who have given it to her—then she is not only safe, she is at rest also; although judgment is still before her, and ever approaching nearer, she can meet it (as far as she herself is concerned) in unruffled peace. Is it not more than a faint type of those Thessalonians of long afterward, who turned to God from idols, to serve the living and true God, and to wait for His Son from heaven, even Jesus, who delivered them from the coming wrath?

Let us look at this token closer—this line of scarlet thread, under the security of which, not Rahab only, but her whole house, abide. Some of us know at once, and know well, what it refers to, and have no doubt at all that here we have one of those allusions, always recurring, to what was always in the mind of God from the beginning —to what the ages were hastening on to as their foreordained completion—to what divides in two all human history, as it divides the human race itself—the *blood*, the precious *blood of Christ.* The more you look, however, the more certain and significant does the type appear.

That scarlet line was the sign of a life given up, however lowly a one—a lowliness which has itself significance. It was the product of death; although but a worm it might be, and was, that died. Death none the less provided the token of salvation for Rahab, as for us the death of Another has furnished us with the certain pledge of ours.

Nothing but death would do, and that not a natural death, as men speak, but a death surely most of all unnatural—a violent death, at man's hand deliberate murder, but Godward a sacrificial death, in which the innocent paid the debt of the guilty, the just died in behalf of the unjust. This is that which saves us, and alone saves us.

But we can trace this further, and find in the very fact of the death of a *worm*, a parallel with the death of the Lord of glory which should make us bow our heads in adoring worship. Who speaks really in the 22d Psalm? Who knows not, as we cite its opening words—words that find their echo and application in the New Testament alone?

" My God, my God, why hast Thou forsaken me? Why art Thou so far from helping me, and from the words of my roaring? O my God, I cry in the daytime, and Thou hearest not; and in the night season, and am not silent!

" But Thou art holy, O Thou that inhabitest the praises of Israel.

" Our fathers trusted in Thee; they trusted, and Thou

didst deliver them. They cried unto Thee, and were delivered; they trusted in Thee, and were not confounded. *But I am a worm*, and no man!"

Who is this holy Sufferer? Who is it that justifies God in the midst of (as far as himself was considered) inexplicable abandonment? Who is it that is the one solitary exception to all God's ways with the righteous?—righteous above all, and yet forsaken, as no righteous person ever was beside?

Yes, it is the Lord, the Life-giver, the Saviour! It is the Highest in the place of the lowest! Lower than man —a worm—but oh, for what, but that the token of salvation might be ours?—the pledge of a mercy which puts those who take shelter under it in absolute and assured security, and gives, with Rahab, "boldness in the day of judgment" itself!

Christ had to take that awful place of a worm and no man; not treated as other men, but apart from all that was natural in God's holy ways of government. For when were the righteous forsaken? Never! They had gone through death, but they had gone through it with God, with the Lord as their Shepherd, fearing no evil, His rod and His staff their comfort. But when the Lord went through it, over whom death had no title at all, it was a totally different thing. That cloud of darkness that hung over the cross was but a symbol of deeper darkness which pressed upon the soul of Him who made atonement for our sins there. It was not that, as a very beautiful hymn says, but here misinterpreting, "The darkness sought His woes to hide;" here it was rather our darkness, the due of our sins, which fell upon Him who bore them for us, and blotted out the sun at midday: the terrible shadow of our curse borne, and needed to be borne, by Him who was made a curse for us.

But Rahab has more than the scarlet thread. Indeed, of what use would this be to her, if she had not her pledged and living witnesses in the camp of Israel? After all, her hope must be in the living, not the dead. Death alone would not do as her security, if she had not the living as witness in her behalf. And so it is again with us. Not only Christ has died—He who died liveth! Risen and gone up on high, His life is the pledge of our life: "Because I live," says He to His disciples, "ye shall live also." "If when we were enemies, we were reconciled to God by the death of His Son, much more, being reconciled, we shall be saved by His *life*."

It is a living Saviour who thus makes good to us the value of His death. It is One who has not only pledged His life for us, as the spies did theirs for Rahab, but has laid it actually down, and whose resurrection is the assurance of His work being accepted for us. It is His voice still which speaks from heaven—the old invitation, the old assurances which He gave on earth, but now with a love no more straitened in its expression. It is not only of forgiveness He can now speak, but of justification—of acquittal; for we are "justified by His blood," and His blood has been shed. "Through this Man is," therefore, "preached unto you the forgiveness of sins; and by Him all that believe are justified from all things, from which ye could not be justified by the law of Moses." (Acts xiii. 38, 39.)

Wonderful it is for sinners such as we are to be forgiven—more wonderful, a great deal, for sinners to be justified. As forgiven, God's mercy reaches out its hand to us; but as justified, His righteousness shields and covers us. God, with all that He is, is for us. Himself is our "hiding-place." What arrow of the enemy can pierce through such a defence?

He who has been in death as the due of our sins has been raised up from the dead by the glory of the Father. The brightness in the face of Him who represents us to God is the assurance of how complete has been the putting away of cloud and distance between us who believe and God. The two spies back in the camp of Israel were Rahab's security: how secure are we, who have our pledge in the risen Saviour at the right hand of God!

When judgment should fall upon the devoted city of Jericho, then would appear how safely the scarlet line could protect Rahab's house of refuge. The crash of Jericho's walls would only be to her the announcement of deliverance, complete and final. The time of the world's judgment will be for us the time when we, too, shall be displayed in the full completeness of our salvation.

But let me guard against a possible mistake here. We must not imagine that we have to wait for the day of judgment in order to realize salvation for ourselves. Rahab had indeed to wait for it; but in applying the figure here, we must remember that faith anticipates and substantiates to us things not seen as yet, and that, for faith, the cross of Christ is already the judgment of the world. So the Lord expressly says: "Now is the judgment of this world; and I, if I be lifted up from the earth, will draw all men unto Me." Rahab's deliverance then more closely represents to us how the world's judgment is passed through and escaped. The cross is both the judgment of the world and our salvation.

Faith can see judgment passed over already, and realize already deliverance out of a present evil world, To it we belong no more—no more of the world than Christ is of the world.

Just as it was in the night of the Passover, when the

blood of the Lamb was put upon the door-post, and Israel, in order to their first step out of Egypt, had to learn the shelter of the blood, to see the judgment upon Egypt come and roll over, and to know it passed and gone, and themselves saved.

Christ's death for us is what Scripture teaches us to reckon as *our* death, and by that death with Him to know ourselves free from condemnation;—dead to sin, to law, and to the world. We look back on judgment, and not forward to it. We have heard the blessed words of Him by whom alone God will at last judge the world, saying, "He that heareth My words, and believeth on Him that sent Me, hath everlasting life, *and shall not come into judgment*" (so the words really read), "but is passed from death unto life." (John v. 24.)

Thus furnished, we start upon our journey. God's perfect love casts out fear for him that is perfect in the lesson He would teach us. For "herein is love made perfect with us, that we should have boldness in the day of judgment, because as He is, so are we in this world." (1 John iv. 17, *margin*.) As He is,—Christ, who is now with God,—so are we. And when He comes to judge the world, we shall be, not shut up with Rahab within the walls of the doomed place, but rather, like the liberated spies, in the army of the Avenger. "Know ye not that the saints shall judge the world?"

But let us return for a short time to Rahab's house within the walls. How beautiful that request of hers for all her house! How sweet the grace that invites now all within the City of Destruction to take refuge where the scarlet line protects equally all who take refuge there. In the house or outside it, that was the only question. The different conditions, experiences, feelings, aye, or degrees of guilt or of goodness, found among those assembled there had naught to do with their safety. Salvation was the common lot and portion of all of them. They were saved by that scarlet line in the window, and not by anything in themselves at all. Every one is welcome, invited, besought to take shelter under the precious blood of Christ. It is not a question of our thoughts, or our feelings, or our experiences; no, it is not any question even of faith, except just so far as this: that it be faith sufficient to carry us there where the only effectual shelter is to be found. No way to God is there but by Christ; no faith, save faith in Him, will avail at all. And thus God preaches to us in this wonderful way, in these records of the past, what He is just now telling us so plainly in the gospel. These types are so precious because in them the God of the Old Testament and the God of the New are so plainly one. Thus He would press upon us what He is, and invite our hearts to confidence in Him.

And oh, if we reject the loving mercy which has cost Him so dear—the loving mercy which He delights to show—what will it be for us when, unsheltered and unsaved, we have to meet God in wrath and judgment? The scarlet line was no safeguard for the city at large; the cross of Christ, whatever the dreams of dreamers, is none for the world. There was one place of refuge only, where an insignificant scarlet thread was proclaimed, in a woman's story, a safer trust than the city walls. The very house was itself upon the wall; who could have supposed that a line of scarlet thread would hold up the house when the wall fell?

And the cross is foolishness as great to men. Why should faith in it have so much virtue? Yet the foolishness of God is wiser than men.

How will it be with you? I want you to realize, beloved friends, while we are speaking here so quietly, yet that judgment is surely, silently coming nearer on the wings of each passing moment. Up to the very time when it took its course in Jericho, the people held out defiantly. They quaked, no doubt, when they heard of the Jordan passage; but after that, what took place would only reassure them. Seven days of mere marching round a wall, and blowing trumpets! Did it not look like consciousness of utter impotence in face of these walls, of which they had long ago spoken so hopelessly? Yet at the word of the Lord those walls fell flat, and judgment came upon all but those saved by the sheltering token of the scarlet line.

Will you accept that foolishness of God which is wiser than men? or will you take your refuge in human wisdom, to prove its folly? The Lord grant that you may realize that salvation which is offered to you to-night freely! It has cost God an infinite deal; it will cost you nothing, because you could not possibly contribute to its purchase. Will you, beloved friends, to-night accept it? God only knows when the end will be—when the last trump will be sounded—when the last word, so to speak, of reconciliation will be uttered—when the Master of the house will rise up and shut to the door. Then, with doom in view, it will be vain to say, "Lord, Lord, open to us!" Your lips will utter that cry when too late.

How solemn to think that it may be so with some now here! The Lord grant in His grace that that story of old may speak to your souls to-night, and that you may find shelter under that precious blood of Christ, of which Rahab's scarlet thread is only the type and pattern!

# THE DEMONIAC.

(Mark v. 1-20.)

"THAT which doth make manifest is light." The presence of Jesus in the world made manifest its true condition. The various forms of human wretchedness which met His eye and were ministered to by His hand, were not, in general, unwonted or exceptional forms. Each had its place, and each gave some distinctive feature to the picture of our poor fallen humanity as it lies around us at this very hour. And therein lies for us much of the blessedness of watching our Lord's ways amid a scene like this, where sins and sorrows like our own meet not mere exposure but relief from Him, in whom, as God manifest, "light" and "love" are one.

The story before us may be pleaded, however, as an exception, in some measure, to this. Without delaying to reason as to it, I desire to point out how, when we look somewhat deeper than the surface, we shall find still what has direct reference and application to ourselves, to the condition of the world—of man at large. But here, as commonly enough, that which is external and bodily is made the type of spiritual and internal things.

"And when He was come out of the ship, immediately there met him out of the tombs a man with an unclean spirit, who had his dwelling among the tombs, and no man could bind him—no, not with chains: because that he had been often bound with fetters and chains, and the chains had been plucked asunder, and the fetters broken in pieces; neither could any man tame him. And always, night and day, he was in the mountains and in the tombs, crying, and cutting himself with stones."

How terrible a picture of the power of Satan over man! How still more terrible to find under this bodily possession the type of a spiritual power exercised far and wide over those in whom, as "children of disobedience," the "god of this world" works! There are some features strongly enough marked here to identify this working, wherever found.

1. He "had his dwelling among the tombs." The place of death and corruption is Satan's familiar haunt. He delights in the ruin his hands have wrought. But how manifestly his triumph over man is seen, when he can inspire his infatuated victim with his own tastes, and make him a willing captive in the scene of his own degradation. But you think, perchance, reader, "this does not apply to me, however." Of that you must judge for yourself, of course. Certain I am, for my part, that this earth we tread is far less the home of the living than of the dead. Its buried generations lie thickly strewn around us. Death is the seal and stamp of God upon a scene which sin has blighted. And from man to the worm of the dust, from the cedar of Lebanon to the hyssop upon the wall, the creature is made subject to vanity. All die. "Sin has reigned unto death."

And thus we are not, when our eyes are opened, "dwellers," but sojourners. "The world passeth away." It is so plain a fact that it would not be thought necessary for any to be reminded of it, even for a moment. As the Psalmist says, man "seeth that wise men die, likewise the fool and the brutish person perish, and leave their wealth to others." Yet what does he add as to those who see this? "Their inward thought is that their houses shall continue forever, and their dwelling-places to all generations; they call the lands after their own names. Nevertheless, man being in honor abideth not; he is like the beasts that perish. This their way is their folly; *yet their posterity approve their sayings.*" (Ps. xlix. 10–13.) Thus man takes possession of what he cannot keep. In his heart he is a "dweller," where even for sight and sense he is a sojourner only; and although God has come in with the proffer of eternal life, and opened heaven to the outcasts of earth, alas, little attraction is there for men in general. They are still characteristically dwellers among the tombs, and their wisdom approves itself not as that which "descendeth from above," but as what is "*earthly, sensual, devilish.*" (Jas. iii. 15.) "Devilish"!—for what evidence of being under Satan's power could there be more, than when dying men cling to a dying world in spite of very sight and sense, of reason and self-interest alike? when they would sooner have their toilsome, careworn life, grey hairs and furrowed brows, and disappointments and bereavements all together, than the heaven they so often say they *hope for*, but, I fear me, only as the one alternative with hell? Have you your "dwelling among the tombs," reader? not loving them, of course, but your heart knowing no better portion than a home in the valley of the shadow of death—in a world which passeth away, and the lust thereof? If so, how little are you different from this poor demoniac of Gadara, save that the devil that had possession of *his body*, has (alas) possession of *your* SOUL?

2. But look now at the second characteristic. "And no man could bind him; no, not with chains; because that he had been often bound with fetters and chains, and the chains had been plucked asunder by him, and the

fetters broken in pieces, neither could any man tame him." Just such, once more, are men. Not this man or that man, but men in general. For what are laws, all laws, human or divine, but chains and fetters cast round men?—chains that they often break; but without them, who would trust another? Take the most plausible advocate of the goodness of human nature; watch him in his dealings with others, and you will soon find what real confidence he has in the goodness which he vaunts. How many of his neighbors will he trust with twenty dollars without good security? and how many of his neighbors would trust *him?* But take away the restraint of law, and who would trust himself unarmed upon the public road? You will perhaps say, it is of the exceptionally bad we should have cause to be afraid; but all experience proves you would soon scarce know whom to trust. And Scripture confirms this with its simple, broad, decisive statements: "As in water face answereth to face, so the heart of man to man." Who has not "lusts?" With opportunity to gratify lust, and fear of punishment removed, how long would men desist to gratify those lusts? "As it is written, There is none righteous, no, not one; there is none that understandeth, there is none that seeketh after God; they are all gone out of the way, they are together become unprofitable, there is none that doeth good, no, not one. Their throat is an open sepulchre; with their tongues they have used deceit; the poison of asps is under their lips; whose mouth is full of cursing and bitterness; their feet are swift to shed blood; destruction and misery are in their ways; and the way of peace have they not known; there is no fear of God before their eyes." "Now we know that whatsoever things the law saith, it saith to them that are under the law, that EVERY mouth may be stopped, and ALL THE WORLD become guilty before God." How vain, then, to plead exception for any! But—

3. "Neither could any man tame him." What do the efforts of men in this respect amount to? Alas, how do they proclaim their utter disbelief of all attempts of this kind, who assert that if you preach to man on God's part, and from His love alone, the free gift of a complete, a present, and an eternal salvation, then you open the floodgates of immorality at once. And though this is only the blindness of unbelief, how can they more tell out their inmost thought that man can never be tamed—no, not by all the love that God can show man, but that he must be bound with fetters and chains, with the restraint of fear of the day of judgment, because he never can be converted to the pure love of God and good?

4. And always, night and day, he was in the mountains, and in the tombs, crying, and cutting himself with stones." What a spectacle of utter misery! And even so, men are moral suicides. What more common than the expression, "He was an enemy to nobody except himself"? And though that is not true of any, for none can injure himself without injuring others, still it is ever true, that of all enemies, a man's worst one is himself. Indeed, without our own help, no enemy could injure us. Our fleshly lusts, our self-righteousness, our unbelief, with the thousand other evil growths that intertwine themselves with these, are our most real and deadly foes. And whether "in the mountains" of spiritual pride and self-sufficiency, or "in the tombs," the abodes of more palpable corruption, "crying, and cutting himself with stones" is still man's most constant occupation. It is a terrible picture, but a most true and lifelike one. Every " child of disobedience" is one in whom "the prince of the power of the air" thus "worketh."

But we are now to look at the demoniac's deliverance. "But when he saw Jesus afar off, he ran and worshiped him." That it was not the devil brought him to the feet of Jesus we may be quite sure; and we may get in this more than a hint of how the devil's power is exercised over those in whom he works. It is not the direct might and mastery of a superior being. Mere force this way would not be suffered. But even if "the god of this world blinds the mind, lest the light of the glorious gospel\* of Christ shines in," it is only the minds of "those that *believe* not," and who thus by the rejection of God's grace and love shut themselves up under Satan's power. It is not that the Word is not witness to itself. It is not that the light shining is not evidence for all. No: the condemnation is that "light is come into the world, and men *loved* darkness rather than light." Not that they were ignorant that the light was there; but they loved and chose darkness. Will was at work, and the heart rejecting. Thus man yields himself up to the devil, and then and thus his blinding power is exercised, until the deluded soul finds perhaps a hundred good reasons for rejecting what he never wanted to receive. How little conscious we are of how the understanding is controlled by the will, and how men may end by becoming "honest infidels" to the truth, who yet never became so in an honest way.

With Jesus in the scene, the power of Satan is broken. "When he saw Jesus afar off, he ran and worshiped him." Reader, have you ever done so? Of course, I do not mean, do you go to church on Sunday, or "say your prayers." But I mean, have you ever in your heart of hearts owned and bowed to the One whom man has re-

---

\* Rather, "the gospel of the glory of Christ."

jected, and whom God has put at His right hand in glory? Your salvation lies in this, for "whosoever shall call upon the name of the Lord shall be saved." The way out of Satan's power is in the truthful acknowledging of Him who was manifested that "He might destroy the works of the devil." Put yourself under His authority and power, and He will manifest it on your behalf and for your deliverance. "Come unto me," says He, "all ye that labor and are heavy laden, and I WILL give you rest."

But in a strange way does the poor victim approach the Lord: "And cried, saying, What have I to do with thee, Jesus, thou Son of the most high God? I adjure thee by God that thou torment me not." Here is the devil and the man's voice mingled, and in such a way you cannot distinguish them. And with how many to whom the Lord has been saying, as we learn He had been here, "Come out of the man, thou unclean spirit," is this the case? For how many come, beseeching Him, the Deliverer, "not to torment them!" With an awakened conscience, and the meaning of the cross not seen, how natural the thought that the holy and the just God must be against them! And how much positive influence of Satan, too, is there in this, when He has so distinctly declared His grace, and justified it by a work done for sinners, and for sinners only! Oh that every one did fully understand that it is Satan's work to impute enmity to the good and gracious God, who gave His Son for us, as if *He* needed to be "reconciled," or have His heart changed toward us, whereas it is *we*, not He, that need the reconciliation. Reader, the "just God" and the "Saviour" are One. The righteousness of God is revealed in the gospel—in good news to men. God has got title to show out His love to us by the cross; and sin

## THE DEMONIAC. 69

is no hindrance to the blessing of those that come to Him, for Christ died for sinners.

"And He asked him, What is thy name? And he answered, saying, My name is Legion, for we are many. And he besought Him much that He would not send them away out of the country." Then follows a solemn word. "Now there was there, nigh unto the mountains, a great herd of swine feeding. And all the devils besought Him, saying, Send us into the swine, that we may enter into them. And forthwith Jesus gave them leave."

The solemn thing is that men (though not all men) are called "swine" in Scripture. "Give not that which is holy unto dogs, neither cast ye your pearls before *swine*, lest they trample them under their feet, and turn again, and rend you." Again, "It is happened unto them according to the true proverb, The dog is turned to his own vomit again, and the sow that was washed to her wallowing in the mire." Thus the "swine" are those who, possessed of their own sensual lusts, value not the precious things of God, though presented to them. Such may have had "the knowledge of the Lord and Saviour Jesus Christ" (2 Pet. ii. 20), though never so as to change the nature, but only skin deep, washing off the pollutions of the world without, but not reaching to the corruption of the heart within (comp. ch. i. 14); leaving the swine still swine, and, of course, finally to go back to wallowing in the mire once more. How many such there are, in the heat of so-called "revivals," whether true or false, converted, as they thought, to God, but who in result are found only to have known enough of "religion," to make light of it altogether. In many cases, too, false teaching gives its help to persuade them that it was real conversion they had, though it was not able to keep them out of the world six months, nay, one month, or a week. Thus they can the more thoroughly despise it, knowing the poor, worthless thing it was to them. But how solemn this backsliding when we see in it, as Peter speaks, the manifestation of the swine's nature, and contemplate their "latter end, worse with them than the beginning." And what more appalling than even the hint, if you will call it no more, that is given by this narrative, that they may be as he out of whom the devil went, but only to return with seven others more wicked than himself, to enter in and dwell there! "And forthwith Jesus gave them leave. And the unclean spirits went out and entered into the swine; and the herd ran violently down a steep place into the sea, and were choked in the sea."

Reader, if you be a rejector of God's precious truth, beware! Is it impossible that He whom thou rejectest may leave thee to manifest the awful reality of Satan's power, driven, for the warning of others, headlong to destruction?

Yet let me say, if the voice of Jesus lingers in your ears—if you are not yet deaf to it utterly—still it says, "Come," and you may come; and still, whosoever cometh, He will in no wise cast out.

"And they that fed the swine fled, and told it in the city, and in the country. And they went out to see what it was that was done. And they come to Jesus, and see him that was possessed with the devil, and had the legion, *sitting*, and *clothed*, and *in his right mind*." What a contrast in every feature to the man he was! the shame of nakedness removed; the restless wandering changed to peace; the untamed maniac, a terror to all around, now in the quiet possession of himself; the company of Satan changed for the sweet companionship of the Son of God. Oh, to have in our soul the deep reality of all these blessings! Reader, in their fullest meaning, they are the portion, every one of them, of him who has come to Jesus. If you have done so, come and count over the jewels in thy casket; if thou hast not come, still the Lord keeps all this for thee; if thou covet it, it may be thine.

"Sitting."

For He giveth rest. Himself has done all, finished all—proclaimed it "finished." The grace of God *brings* salvation, consequently, to all men. (Tit. ii. 11.) You have not to work for it, but to take it. If you *have* come, He has received you. You may say, I have not rest; but you have title to it and His word must be your assurance, *not* your feelings, that He has received you. He casts out NONE, not *you* then. Take His word for it, and you will rest.

"Clothed."

"Behold," says the angel of the Lord to Joshua (Zech. iii. 4), "I have caused thine iniquity to pass from thee, and I will clothe thee with change of raiment." It is God's own hand furnishes this clothing, and clothes with it, too. "The best robe" comes to us from the Father's hand and love. "He hath covered me with the robe of righteousness." "All *our* righteousnesses are as filthy rags;" but Christ "is of God made unto us righteousness." (Isa. lxi. 10; lxiv. 6; 1 Cor. i. 30.)

To those who believe, then, Christ is made over. God appropriates Him to them, that the shame of their nakedness may not appear. They are "in Christ" before God, and His beauty and glory are seen upon them. Not only is there "no condemnation," but they are "accepted in the Beloved" (Eph. i. 6), and "as He is, so are they even in this world." (1 John iv. 17.)

One more blessedness of this cleansed and delivered man of Gadara: he was—

"In his right mind."

For, reader, however "their posterity approve their sayings," the "way" of the men of this world, wise in their generation as they may be, is "folly," and none but he who has Christ has really "wisdom." If you think not so yet, a few steps more upon the road you are taking, and you will be convinced of it. The opened eye of faith alone sees things as they are. God's estimate of the world will stand. The things "seen" are but "temporal;" the things "unseen" are yet "eternal." "It is appointed unto men once to die, and after this the judgment." Happy and wise alone is he who can say with the apostle, "I count all things but loss for the excellency of the knowledge of Christ Jesus my Lord." "He that drinketh of the water that I shall give him," says the Lord himself, "shall never thirst."

"And they were afraid . . . and they began to pray him to depart out of their coasts." Were these in their right mind, alas? Do you know that many who are in like manner respectful to the Lord, are only yet praying Him to leave them to the devil? Do you know that multitudes of so-called Christian worshipers, are only respectfully bowing Him out of their houses and hearts? Do you know that for multitudes (to change the figure), Christ is but a dressed-up image to be worshiped in the churches, and left there till the next occasion? not the living One, not the gracious Master and Lord, not the Friend that sticketh closer than a brother, not the companion of the heart and life? And do you know, that in such cases the only *true* prayer they ever make Him is, "Depart from us; for we desire not the knowledge of thy ways?" How different with the really delivered soul: "And when He was come into the ship, he that had been possessed with the devil prayed Him that He might be with Him." And this desire is of Himself, and shall be fully satisfied. We shall be "ever with the Lord." Before that day comes there is a brief but blessed interval of service given: "Howbeit Jesus suffered him not, but saith unto him, Go home to thy friends, and tell them how great things the Lord hath done for thee, and hath had compassion on thee. And he departed, and began to publish in Decapolis how great things Jesus had done for him; and all men did marvel."

May such be the testimony rendered to the Lord Jesus, dear reader, by you and me!

# THE GOSPEL IN THE GENEALOGY.

(Matt. i. 1-6.)

"And Judas begat Pharez and Zara of Thamar; . . . and Salmon begat Booz of Rahab; and Booz begat Obed of Ruth; and David the king begat Solomon of her that had been the wife of Urias."

THE introduction of four women's names, and of four only, into the genealogy of our Lord as given by Matthew, has furnished material for inquiry to many students of the inspired word. That there was a special purpose in it no one who had any right claim to be such could ever doubt. Moreover, a slight glance only at the names so chosen to a place in connection with the human descent of the Lord of Glory would show something of the significance of their being found there. They are precisely such names as a chronicler, left to mere human wisdom in the matter, and especially a Jew, however right thinking, would have kept out of sight; and especially so as there was no apparent necessity for bringing them forward. They were not needed at all as establishing the connection of our Lord with David or with Abraham. No other names of women are thus introduced—neither Sarah, Rebekah, Leah, nor any other; while yet there was perhaps not another who might not seem to have better title to be remembered. These women were of all others, though in different ways, just the blots apparently upon the genealogy. And then, so far from any attempt at concealment of what was discreditable in connection with them, circumstances which needed not (one might have thought) to be referred to, are brought in, as if to draw our attention to what otherwise might have been less noticed. Thus Zara's twin-birth with Pharez, though himself not in the line of the genealogy, is mentioned as if to recall the circumstances of that sin which brought them into being; while Bathsheba, instead of being mentioned by name, is associated, as it were, with all the horror of the crimes which her name alone one would think sufficient to bring to mind —"her that had been the wife of Urias."

But there is something very beautiful as well as characteristic in this fearlessness of one who, here as in other places—in a mere record of names, as it might seem, as well as in the most solemn passages of our Lord's life— spake as he was moved by the Holy Ghost. If there be a blot upon the life of one of His people, the God of truth will never hesitate to bring it out, though it might seem to be furnishing an occasion to those who seek occasion against the truth; and if there be a dark spot that presumptuous man would dare to lay a finger on, on but one of the links (each divinely constituted) of the chain of ancestry of the Man Christ Jesus, the Spirit of God puts *His* finger upon it first, to invite our attention to it as something worthy of being noted, and calculated only, in the mind of faith, to beget reverential thoughts and lowly admiration of a wisdom that never fails, and that is most itself when it confounds all other.

Now to a faith that (as is characteristic of it) "believeth on Him that justifieth the ungodly," the introduction of the names of Tamar and of Bathsheba into the inspired record of the Lord's human ancestry, is pregnant with suggestions fitted to awaken the liveliest emotion. Each of these women of dishonored names and shameful memories had title, then, in a peculiar way, to appropriate those words which recorded Israel's most real boast: "Unto us a child is born, unto us a son is given." The human feeling—for there is that in it whatever there may be more—which has given an "immaculate conception" to the mother of our Lord, would have at least provided for the unblemished character of the line of His natural descent; and that feeling would have said, Let Him have connection with the purest and noblest only that can be found; and thus it is that human thought has been shown folly in the wisdom of One who, from the beginning, took the "seed of the *woman*"—first as she had been in the transgression—to bruise the serpent's head, and heal those that are oppressed of the devil. Fixed, in divine wisdom, in that part of our Saviour's genealogy which no Jew could dispute—for none could dispute that the Christ was to come of David—these names (all perhaps Gentile, and some undoubtedly so) stood there to vindicate the Gentiles' part in the "child born." And just so in the face of pretension to human righteousness they stood to vindicate the claims of *sinners* to Him whose "body was prepared Him" that He might die for sinners.

Thus far, then, the meaning of these names in the connection in which we find them is plain enough, and their place in the genealogy not only needs no vindication, but is another note of harmony in that song of praise which His word, as well as all other of His works, is perpetually singing—seed to sow music in the hearts of the sorrowful, in the assurance of how the sighing of the prisoners has come up before the Lord.

But what if we are able to go further and to show that not only is this so but that each of the four names here given furnishes its own peculiar feature to what, taken as a whole, is really a full and blessed declaration of the story of grace and of salvation—each in its order adding what the former had left out, till the whole is told? Would it not be worthy of God to speak so—to make not only types and parables, but the very names of a genealogy repeat a story He is never weary of telling, however slow man may be to hear?

Let us take up, then, the history of these four names, so far as it connects them with this inspired genealogy, and try to read the lesson which is given us by their connection with it.

The history of Tamar you will find in Genesis xxxviii. It is one of those dark chapters of human depravity which the Word lays open with its accustomed plainness and outspokenness. Infidels would speak of it as a blot upon the book that contains it, and few perhaps care to read it, least of all aloud. And yet it is a story that will one day again find utterance before the most magnificent assembly that the earth or the heavens ever saw or shall see. And how many such like stories shall come out then—mine, reader, and yours, not perhaps, after all, so far removed from Tamar's—and the pure eternal day will not withdraw its beams, and the night not cover it up with its darkness.

What must be told *then*, may well bear to be told *now*. The light that shines upon evil deeds is all undefiled by them. If Tamar's history were a mere thing of the past and had no voice for succeeding generations, no doubt it had been vain to bring it up; but now let us rather thank Him for doing it, who has given us a page of human history so dark that we have to shudder; so filthy that we have to blush at it. Reader, I ask again, is there no page of *your* life, that, if it were written by the faithful hand of God, you would have to blush at in like manner?

Now, in all this history of Tamar's, the thing that

strikes me in this connection is, that there is no redeeming feature about it. If I take the record attached to the other names which have place with hers in this genealogy, I may find perhaps in each case something that breaks the darkness a little. But I find nothing similar recorded about Tamar. She comes before me in this picture as a sinner and nothing else. The wife successively of two men, each cut off for his wickedness by divine judgment, she dares yet in her own person, by crime equal to theirs, provoke divine judgment. But the wonder above all this is, that it is this very sin that brings her name into the Lord's genealogy—for this sin it was that made her the mother of Pharez, one of the direct line in Christ's ancestry.

Is there no voice in this? And is it the voice of the God of judgment, or is it the voice of the God of grace, the God and Father, indeed, of our Lord Jesus Christ? True, if I look alone at the Old-Testament record, it may call up before me, as it has called up, the time of account and manifestation; but the moment I turn to the New Testament and find Tamar first of women's names in the genealogy of the Lord—Tamar, *brought in by her sin into that connection*—I find what fixes my mind upon a scene of judgment, indeed, and that of the most solemn sort, but where the Holy One of God stands for the unholy, where Barabbas's cross—place of the chief of sinners—bears the burden of One who alone bare all our burdens, and "with whose stripes we are healed."

Oh, blessed lesson, and worthy of God to give! Tamar's sin her connection with the Lord of life and glory? and O beloved, look! was not our sin our connection? Did not He die for sinners? Was it not when we confessed our sins, and, with our mouths stopped, took our places before God, ungodly and without strength, that we found out the wondrous fact that for the ungodly and without strength Christ had died; and that *because* we were sinners, and Christ had died for such, He was "faithful and just to forgive us our sins and to cleanse us from all unrighteousness"?

Thus Tamar's name, first in this genealogy, is first also in the simple gospel truth that it reveals; and the fact that Tamar is a sinner, of whom I can read nothing but her sin, and whose sin gives her connection in a peculiar way with the Christ who came for sinners, is light and joy and gladness in my soul.

But we must turn to Rahab.

And here again we are not in very creditable company. Rahab is a Canaanite, one of a cursed race, and Rahab is a harlot, sinner among sinners. We seem destined to move in this track. The one thing recorded to her advantage is her faith. That it had fruit too, none can question. She is one whom the apostle James takes up, to ask us, "Was not Rahab, the harlot, justified by works, when she had received the messengers, and sent them out another way"? But even here, you will observe, the thing he appeals to is not what would, in men's eyes, make a saint of her. There was no brilliance of devotedness, no wonderful self-sacrifice, no great *goodness*, as one might say. Even in the very thing in which she shows her faith she tells a lie; as if to isolate faith from any kind of merit whatever, and to give us expressly the picture of one that "worketh *not*," but whose only hope is in a God who "justifieth the ungodly." (Rom. iv. 5.)

And who can doubt it was Rabah's *faith* that brought her into the genealogy, as *sin* had brought Tamar? Without faith, she had died with those shut up in Jericho, a cursed woman of a cursed race. Faith removed that curse from her; faith brought her in among the people of

God, if it did not attract to her the heart of Salmon, so as in the most direct way to account for those words being in the genealogy, "Salmon begat Booz of Rachab."

Thus the second of these women's names teaches us a lesson as sweet and as needful as the former. "To him that worketh not, but believeth" is what we instinctively think of when we think of Rahab,—faith that, while it has that which demonstrates its reality, leaves one still to be justified as ungodly, nay, believes on One who only does so justify,—faith which looks not at itself, therefore, and pleads not its own performances, but brings the soul to accept the place of ungodliness only, because for the ungodly only there is justification.

This is very sweet and very wonderful. It is wonderful to find how in the mere introduction of a name into a catalogue, the God of grace can speak out the thoughts of His own heart. And it is very sweet to see how constantly before Him is the thought of our need and of His mercy, and how He would by the very wonder, as it were, surprise men's slow, cold hearts into the belief of it.

And now we have got to Ruth: "Booz begat Obed of Ruth."

But what shall we say of Ruth? Here at first sight our text might seem to fail us, and we might seem to have parted company with sinners. Why, you might say, the Spirit of God Himself takes a whole book to tell us about Ruth. And true, indeed though it be that she was a Gentile, as Rahab and as Tamar, you might repeat of her what the Lord Himself says of another Gentile: "I have not found so great faith, no, not in Israel." With no sword of judgment hanging over her head as over Rahab's, with no tie to connect her with Israel but the memory of a dead husband who had himself abandoned it, with the memory of famine in that land which had forced her husband out, and with the company only of an aged woman, with whom bitter providences, as she deems them, have changed the name of Naomi into Mara, Ruth comes into the land and to the God of Israel, in whose fields she is content to be a gleaner. No, do not think, reader, that I would disparage the worth, or blot the fair fame of Ruth the Moabitess. That she was a Gentile only adds to it the more honor, in that among the godless grew her godliness, and that she was faithful where Israel's own children had set her the example of unfaithfulness.

But is there nothing in this very fact that, in company with the names of sinners among sinners, we find one who shines, as it were, saint among saints? What does it mean, this putting down of Ruth in company with such names as Tamar, Rahab, Bathsheba? Is it not a truth of the same kind as when the Word tells us of one who "gave much alms" and "prayed to God alway," that he was to send to Joppa for a man who should tell him words whereby he should be saved? Or as when Zaccheus, standing forth and saying to the Lord, "Behold, Lord, the half of my goods I give to the poor," meets the significant and gentle word—you can scarcely call it reproof—"This day is SALVATION come to this house, for as much as he also is a son of Abraham; for the Son of Man is come to seek and to *save* that which was LOST."

So that without the smallest word of detraction from Ruth's goodness, but rather allowing in its very fullest all that can be claimed for it, we may fairly draw a lesson from the company in which we find her name, which is itself full of instruction and of beauty; and Tamar, Rahab, Ruth, side by side in the genealogy, give us but the announcement of Isaiah's vision, which the Baptist's mission went to fulfill: "Every valley shall be filled, and every mountain and hill shall be brought low, and all flesh shall see the salvation of God." Yes, God's salvation as much needed, and in the same way, by one as another—as much of grace to one as to another, to Ruth the Moabitess, as to Rahab or Tamar.

But we have not yet got at that which gives fullest significance to this name in the genealogy. Against this Ruth, with all her loveliness and with all her goodness, there was lying a ban which did not lie in the same way against the others. She was a Moabitess, and against these there had been leveled an express statute of the law. "An Ammonite or a Moabite shall not enter into the congregation of the Lord, even unto their tenth generation they shall not enter into the congregation of the Lord *forever*." (Deut. xxiii. 3.) Thus Ruth lay under the interdict of the law. It is striking that it was to this devoted, to this lovely woman that the law applied,—not to Rahab nor even to Tamar; God having thus proclaimed in an unmistakable way the law's character; not bringing it in to condemn the sinner and the harlot, (where men's minds would have done so,) but introducing it as that which would have excluded a Ruth, even with her piety. Emphatically was it thus taught that it was man as *man* that was shut out from God;—not in his sins merely, but in his righteousness; and that if we stand on *that* ground all "our *righteousnesses* are as filthy rags."

But the law does not keep Ruth out. Moabitess as she is, she does enter into the congregation of the Lord. The law is set aside in her behalf, and instead of her descendants being excluded to the tenth generation, her child of the third generation sits upon Israel's throne, and hears the promise which confirms that throne to his heirs for succeeding generations.

Thus another principle comes out in bright relief. If

God takes up the sinner and the harlot on the principle of faith, *law is set aside* by the very fact. "The law is *not* of faith." "The righteousness of God *without the law* is manifested," "even the righteousness of God by faith of Jesus Christ unto all, and upon all them that believe." This is what Ruth is witness to. The Moabitess comes into the congregation of the Lord, spite of the law expressly leveled against her to keep her out; and in this we find but another utterance of this self-same story of grace which, in so many languages, our God so joys to tell.

One name alone remains; one truth has yet to be uttered. God takes up sinners, then, by faith, and law is set aside. "Faith is reckoned for righteousness." Not as if faith *were* righteousness, or its equivalent — that would be quite another thing: but God, who had been looking (to speak humanly) for righteousness by law, had ceased to do so. The law had returned Him answer, "there is *none* righteous; no, not one." Thenceforth the principle was changed. "Faith" was "reckoned for righteousness:" faith that did not pretend to righteousness at all, for it was in One who "justifieth the *ungodly*."

But if God receives sinners, to what does He receive them? Is it a complete salvation they obtain, or are there conditions still to be met before the final goal is reached, and there is complete security? On what, in short, does the *ultimate* salvation of the believer rest? This is a question which evidently needs answering before the soul can be completely satisfied and at peace. It is one thing to be now in the favor of God, and it is another thing to know that I can never lose it. And the more I look at myself, if it depend upon myself, the more I must be in dread of losing it.

Moreover, there are those who will allow of a free *present* salvation, who will not allow of one that gives security absolutely for the future. With them the *sinner* may be saved without works; but the *saint* may not. The legalism shut out at one entrance gains admittance at another, and the result in either case is the same. Self-sufficiency is built up; self-distrust taught to despair; the work of Christ is practically displaced from its office of satisfying the soul, and the grace of God effectually denied.

The Scripture speaks as decidedly on this point as on any other. On justification by the blood of Christ it builds the most confident assurance as to the future. It tells us that inasmuch as "when we were yet sinners Christ died for us, MUCH MORE then, *being now justified by His blood*, WE SHALL BE SAVED from wrath through Him. For if, when we were enemies, we were reconciled to God by the death of His Son, *much more*, being reconciled, we shall be saved by His life." (Rom. v. 8–10.)

And when I turn to this last name of the four, and find "her that had been the wife of Urias" taking her place with Tamar, Rahab, and Ruth in the genealogy of the Lord, it seems as if the text just quoted were repeated in my ears. For, the moment I think of Bathsheba, a greater name than hers, linked strangely with hers in the crime which it recalls, comes in to efface her almost from my mind. David, it is I think of—David, child of God, Israel's sweet psalmist! in whose breathings the souls of saints in every age have poured out their aspirations after "the living God,"—David fallen, and fallen so low that we cannot marvel if his name be side by side with Tamar's. David, man after God's heart! Oh, how many of the Lord's enemies hast thou made to blaspheme! how many of the Lord's people hast thou made to mourn for thee! Was that thy witness to what God's heart approved? Was that thy soul's panting after Him? What! murder a man in the midst of faithful service to thee zealously rendered, that thou mightest hide thine own adultery? Was that the man who, when flying from the face of his enemy, and when Providence had put that enemy within his power, cut off but his skirt, and his heart smote him for it? Ah! sadder than thy heart could be for Saul, we take up thine own lament over thee, "How are the mighty fallen, and the weapons of war perished."

And surely, O Lord our God, in Thy presence shall no flesh glory! If David could not, could we? Alas! if I know myself, what can I do but put my mouth in the dust, and be dumb forever before the Lord! "All flesh is as grass, and all the glory of man as the flower of grass." And "let him that thinketh he standeth take heed lest he fall." The voice that comes to me from David's sin is infinitely more than David's condemnation. It is my own. Can I pretend to be better? Can I take my hand from his blood-stained one? Ah, no! I accept with him my own condemnation; and not as a sinner merely, but as a saint. From first to last, from beginning to end, the voice of David's fall brings to me the assurance that the justification of the ungodly must be my justification still. It is like that voice of God, strange, and contradictory in its utterance, men may call it, which, having pronounced man's sentence before the flood, and destroyed every living thing because "every imagination of the thought of man's heart was only evil continually," after the flood declares, " I will not again curse the ground for man's sake; *for the imagination of man's heart is evil from his youth;* neither will I again smite any more every thing living as I have done."

Blessed be His name! He does not trust His salvation to my hand. My "life" depends but upon the life of Him who has taken His place in heaven, after He had by Himself purged my sins; as much "*for me*" there in the glory as "for me" upon the cross. *He* is the accepted One; I but "in Him." Because He lives, I shall live also.

If David could have taken his salvation out of God's hand, he surely would have done it in the case before us. That he could not I read in this woman's name, partner in his sin, recorded in the genealogy. Once again, as in Tamar's case before, I find sin connecting with the Saviour of sinners. It was not that God did not mark, and in a special way, His abhorrence of the evil. It was only *grace*, really, to do that. "Whatsoever a man soweth that shall he also reap," and no wonder, therefore, if adultery and murder sprung up again and again in David's path. No marvel that the sword never departs from his house, and that his wives are dishonored in the face of the sun. But in the midst of all this growth of thorn and thistle, sure fruit and consequence of sin, one floweret springs up from this cursed ground, type and witness that, where sin had abounded, grace over-abounds. From this David and this Bathsheba, whom sin has united together, a child springs whose name stand next in the line of the ancestry of the Lord; and who receives, as if to confirm this, a special name "Jedidiah," "beloved of the Lord."

And is it an imagination or is it more, that there is something in the name—the other name of this child born —which harmonizes with all this? I will not say; but if Solomon, "peaceful," be a strange name in so near connection with so sad a history, it is not an unsuited one to follow in this genealogical list—not an unsuited one to be in company with Tamar, Rahab, Ruth, or Bathsheba. And it is a blessed one with which to end the history of four names, which when God utters them can be made to speak of what He must love well to utter, or He would scarcely take such strange occasion to remind us of it.

And if to any there seems after all in this, something that seems too much like a mere wonder to be God's utterance, I would beseech such an one to remember how once a burning bush was made just such a wonder to attract a passer-by, and how when he turned aside to see, a voice out of that bush proclaimed that God was really there. Even so may it not be strange that He should attract now by a kind of wonder, to listen to a story which He loves to tell; and for those who turn aside to see, may the same voice, now as then, be heard.

# THE HEALING OF THE ISSUE.

"AND much people followed Him, and thronged Him. And a certain woman which had an issue of blood twelve years, and had suffered many things of many physicians, and spent all that she had, and was nothing bettered, but rather grew worse, when she heard of Jesus, came in the press behind, and touched His garment ; for she said, If I may touch but His clothes I shall be whole. And straightway the fountain of her blood was dried up, and she felt in her body that she was healed of that plague."—MARK V., 24-29.

THAT we should find in the miracles of healing which the Lord wrought upon the body, the types and patterns of spiritual healing, cannot be thought strange This healing of the soul was certainly the great thing in His mind always. That of the body was a display of Divine power soon to pass away. The records remain not only as the witness of that power manifested in goodness among men, and manifesting the glory of the Son of God. According to His own words with regard to the healing of the palsied man, it was that they "might *know* that the Son of Man had power on earth to forgive sin," that He bade him arise, take up his bed, and go unto his house. The bodily healing, which they *could* see, was to be the assurance of the reality of the spiritual healing which they could *not* see.

This, of course, was not saying that the one was actually a type or figure of the other, but it prepares us at

THE HEALING OF THE ISSUE. 89

least to find without much wonder the lesser miracle speak of the greater. Nor must we be surprised that no such interpretation of what is here is given us. The perfection of the picture is that it speaks to the eye for itself without the need of any. Even so has the healing of the bloody issue spoken ever since the day of its record here by one "moved by the Holy Ghost."

The expectation of a miracle had brought for a moment a crowd around the Lord. A ruler of the synagogue had besought Him for his daughter, lying at the point of death. "And Jesus went with him; and much people followed Him and thronged Him." It was for the most part an idle crowd, just such as would be shouting at no distant time, "Away with Him! away with Him! crucify Him!" There is no hint of anything better as to them. Their thronging and pressing upon Him was no good sign, but the reverse. If they "followed Him," it was outside interest, not love or reverence for Him. No "virtue" went out of Him whom they pressed on, for their need, if need they had. They had no real dealing or intercourse with Him at all.

It is very like what is going on at the present day, when, in these professedly Christian times, a crowd is pressing in the self-same way around the Lord. There is much apparent "following." If we look closer, how much through outside influences, how little from real heart for Christ Himself. How few can speak of "virtue" which has come out of Him for them; of eternal life which they have gotten through Him; of justification from all things by His blood.

Amid all this, however, a need that nothing else can meet brings the soul to Christ, and the touch of faith finds virtue in Him as of old. "A certain woman which had an issue of blood twelve years, and had suffered many things of many physicians, and had spent all that she had, and was nothing bettered, but rather grew worse"— how many who read this, perhaps, will say, "That is my picture. How many remedies have I tried for my condition, and I am as far from peace as ever, and more hopeless than ever now of finding it." But let us look at what is here more closely.

"An issue of blood twelve years." A slow, steady, unchecked draining of the life away. A thing not in all its dread significance perceived at once, but surely making itself felt as time goes on, paling the brightness of all the eye looks on and stealing away all vigor of enjoyment, until the pall and shadow of death lies everywhere, and life is labor, and all under the sun is vanity. Know it as we may, or not, this is everywhere a disease we suffer from. Little, if at all, understood in the flush and fervor of youth, when the world is yet untried, its reality gradually, but too soon, steals in upon us. "The world passeth away." There is a doom upon it. Its freshness fades. Its blossoms wither. He that drinketh of this water thirsts again, and it becomes more and more impossible to find even temporary satisfaction from it.

This is the effect of the "issue of blood." It is what sin has wrought. It is the mark of Cain, "a fugitive and a vagabond upon the earth." Everything is fleeting, naught abiding. Death is the palpable mark upon sin. And oh, when the eye is opened, what a world! Could there be aught but death for it? Could it go on, such as it is, forever, under the eye of a holy and good God?

Bnt it is *my* sin that brings the want and weariness and dissatisfaction everywhere into my own soul. It is that I am away from God. For if able to look up out of the midst of it all to One enthroned above it, infinitely good as infinifely great, and with Divine power working out unfailingly the counsels of Divine love,—weariness and unrest would be gone, and acquaintance with Him would give peace, deep and unbroken.

But, alas! when I think of Him, conscience has its tale to tell against me, and cast me off from confidence in Him. My indifference, my enmity to Himself, become in my thoughts the argument (judging Him by myself) that *He* must be careless of or hostile towards me. Sin is upon me, alas, condemning me before Him, and sin is *in* me, accusing Him to my heart; and yet it is with Him I have to do. Here, then, is my issue of blood, draining out of my soul its all of life and joy and satisfaction.

"An issue of blood twelve years!" But that was not all with this poor woman. She "had suffered many things of many physicians." The effort to get relief had thrown her into the hands of those who could accomplish nothing for her, but only added to her affliction. How sure a thing it is, if we have felt anything of *soul*-sickness, that we shall be prone to try any and every invention of man, rather than the Lord's own simple and effectual way of healing. And the equally sure result is, if we are under Divine teaching, that we find suffering instead of healing. God's gospel is the "gospel of peace;" all other gospels fall short of this. Indeed these others are all one at bottom; they bear the marks of one mind from which they all come, for if it is not God's truth we follow, it is the devil's lie.

Thus all men's religious inventions will be found to base themselves upon and suit themselves to the natural thought as to God. They suppose Him against men, and needing to have His heart turned to favor them; and for this purpose some work of man's own needed, to make (as they put it) their peace with Him. Herein is torture enough for a divinely awakened soul. For what is he to do, who has never yet done even his bare duty? How is he to make up for the past, who is for ever adding to his sin? Or if God's mercy will put away the past, still what about this present constant falling short? Will God excuse him again in this? If so, in how much, for this mercy must surely have a limit? "Keep the commandments?" This in the whole he cannot. But "do the best he can;" this too, he finds, he *has* not. Will God,—can He, accept less than even this? Where then draw the line, and upon which side of the line,—accepted or rejected,—does he stand?

Thus all is suffering here, for to such questions there is no answer. Under this system of treatment, if we are in earnest, like the woman in this story, we are "nothing bettered, but rather grow worse." The end is total bankruptcy, and that every way: "she had spent all that she had.

> "None but Jesus
> Can do *helpless sinners* good."

In such a condition there is one advantage, and that a great one: the "many physicians" disappear. For one simply "lost" they have no remedy,—can hold out no further hope. But one physician, and but one method of cure, remains.

What strange faith comes into the soul at the end of so many trials! "When she had heard of Jesus, she came in the press behind, and touched his garment; *for she said, If I may touch but his clothes, I shall be whole.*" What gave her such strange assurance? Just her need. He suited her so well. His grace in its freeness commended itself so to her. He was no vendor of patent medicines, made no profit of the help He brought her. This wondrous prodigality of blessing flowing out of Him for every need was the broad seal of heaven to His commission. It spoke in her heart with all the sweetness of Divine authority, and she gave herself up to the joy it brought, without a doubt.

This is the kinship—so simple, and yet so much misapprehended — between "repentance toward God and faith toward our Lord Jesus Christ." For repentance is indeed that which introduces us to the blessed reality of what He is. We "repent," and we "believe the gospel." Not as if repentance were a legal condition, or legality at all, but, on the contrary, the break-down of it. To "abhor ourselves" with Job is not self-righteousness; it is self-*emptiness*, the conviction of helplessness and evil, to which only the freeness and fullness of the gospel suit. It is not the *doing* of something for God, but the conviction of *inability to do*, which shuts us up to simple receiving of the "*gift* of righteousness." Then how simple indeed faith is, and how suited and sufficient a Saviour Christ becomes!

The faith of the woman with the bloody issue found its answer from the Lord. Faith always does, for all it counts upon Him for. "And straightway the fountain of her blood was dried up, and she *felt in her body* that she was healed of that plague."

Notice how the Lord's healing distinguished itself from all others. It was no lengthy process. He did not put this woman under a course of treatment, as some interpreters of His dealings with the soul would make Him in that case do. No, it was *immediate* healing. "Straightway the fountain of her blood was dried up." How blessed is this! How sure that as to soul-salvation the Lord's way is precisely similar. "Thy sins be forgiven thee" were His first words to the palsied man. "Thy faith hath saved thee," to many another. Nowhere did He put those who came to Him through a probationary course to get their sins forgiven and to find peace with God. And now we are assured in the gospel of a peace *made*,—a " peace *preached*," or proclaimed as made. "*He* is our peace." Faith welcomes this, and enters into it at once.

First faith, *then* feeling; " she *felt* in her body." "Ah," says some one who reads this, "that's what I am waiting for. I want to *feel* that I am healed." But observe, dear reader, *she* did not *wait* to feel. She said, " If I may but touch, I *shall* be healed." She touched, with the assurance that the touch brought healing with it. How much more should you come to Him now with the assurance that *you* are received, when He says, " Him that cometh to me I will in no wise cast out." Come to Him, saying, " I know Thou receivest me," and you will find feeling the result of faith; but if you *wait* for feeling to tell you you are received, you are dishonoring Him by discrediting His word; and how can you expect happy feelings while you are doing so?

Here all is in its place. Her feelings were the honor put upon her faith. She had hold of the blessing, never doubting it was hers, although she had no other assurance but the grace which was flowing out around. We have, on the other hand, the distinct positive word of the Lord that whoever comes to Him is received.

" Immediately the fountain of her blood was dried up." And what a wondrous healing is that with us, when the "salvation of God" makes us to know the "God of salvation." Not against us, as we thought, but having righteous title to show Himself for us through the Cross of Jesus; our "issue of blood" healed by the shedding of the blood of our spotless Substitute. No work of our own sufficing; but no work of our own needed. And all revealed in such unclouded light, that not to have simple certainty of it is unbelief, and sin. How the heart is brought back to God by this wondrous manifestation of what He is, and is to us! He who has given Jesus for us is the One in whose hand all things are. To know this is quietness and assurance of heart.

One word more. In the case of this woman, the Lord claims from her the public acknowledgment of what she had got from Him. She would have stolen the cure and got off unperceived. But no! she must own *Him* now, that He too may own *her* before them all. "Daughter, thy faith hath made thee whole; go in peace, and be whole of thy plague." Let me urge this upon all healed ones, the claim which the Lord makes on them for open confession of Him. It is everything for happiness as Christians to be confessors of Christ, to be open, decided followers of His. It will cost us something before a world which rejects Him still, but it is a small cost, for an infinite gain ; for the principle is always true, "Them that honor Me will I honor." The Lord give us boldness, beloved brethren, and devotedness to Him who has bought us with His precious blood, that we might be a people formed for Himself, to show forth all His praise.

G

# THE FAMINE IN SAMARIA,

AND

## HOW IT WAS RELIEVED.

A GOSPEL ADDRESS. (2 Kings vi. 24–vii.)

WE read here of a famine in Samaria, the capital city of a country most highly favored, most deeply guilty in her abuse of the patience and goodness of a long-suffering God. And now the judgment that must needs overtake iniquity was falling upon her. The enemy was besieging her in her gates, and already we see her in most extreme distress: "they besieged it till an ass's head was sold for fourscore pieces of silver, and the fourth part of a cab of doves' dung for five pieces of silver." In this awful strait, the words of Moses' prophetic denunciation were fulfilled, and that took place which Jeremiah records in his moan of anguish over a still greater calamity, "The hands of the pitiful women have sodden their own children." The king rends his clothes in agony at the terrible disclosure, and the people see sackcloth within upon his flesh; but in the depth of his despair, his heart, really unhumbled, breaks out against God in the person of His prophet: "God do so to me, and more also, if the head of Elisha the son of Shaphat shall stand on him this day." He repents indeed of this rashness, and hastes after his messenger to save the prophet's life, but it is only to break out once more in impatience against God: "Behold, this evil is of the Lord; why should I wait for the Lord any longer?"

Strange it seems to our natural thoughts that just here should come the announcement of blessing: "And Elisha said, 'Hear ye the word of the Lord: thus saith the Lord, To-morrow, about this time, shall a measure of fine flour be sold for a shekel, and two measures of barley for a shekel, in the gate of Samaria.'"

"God's ways are not as our ways, nor His thoughts as our thoughts." No; but because as the heavens are higher than the earth, so are His ways than our ways, and His thoughts than our thoughts. We look at the wickedness of man exhibited here, and we ask "What possible reason could there be here for the coming blessing?" And we can only answer "None, surely; absolutely none." Whatever misery there might be to draw out His pity, goodness there was none to plead on man's behalf; and it was at the very time when the evil which had provoked His judgment was laid fully bare that it pleased God to bring in His mercy. Is there here, then, any exception to His ways? Or is there not here rather a principle of His ways? With an unchangeable God there is no exception. Let us look, then, and see if we can find the principle.

Of God's pity and love we may be sure,— a love that delights ever to come in and show itself,— that must be hindered by some necessity of His holiness if it do *not* show itself in behalf of His needy creatures, whose need should have been but the occasion of their learning more the heart of their Creator. And though sin has brought a dark cloud over all this, God has made this but the background upon which all the brighter the character of His love may be read. His Son has been the messenger and witness of a love that would clasp all in its embrace.

God is showing grace. He has title to show it, apart from any ground in man whatever. It is grace, the essential opposite of works,— of any works at all as a condition: for "if it be of grace, it is no more of works, otherwise grace is no more grace; and if it be of works, it is no more of grace, otherwise work is no more work." It is impossible, then, to mingle these two principles: if you attempt it, the one destroys the other. So, also, of necessity "the law is not of faith." "Not the hearers of the law are just before God, but the doers of the law shall be justified." On the other hand, the gospel-principle is "They that *hear* shall live." Law requires: grace gives. The obedience of the law is giving to God: the obedience of faith is receiving from God. "As many as are of the works of the law are under the curse"; but "Christ hath redeemed us from the curse of the law, being made a curse for us . . . ; that the blessing of Abraham might come upon the Gentiles through Jesus Christ, that we might receive the promise of the Spirit through faith."

But what, then, can hinder the reception of grace? Nothing, surely, but the rejection of it. And is it possible that there should be the rejection of grace? Can God's free gift woo us in vain to its reception? Alas, there is a condition here,— to man the most galling: to receive grace, he must give up self-righteousness. He must humble himself to receive what he has never earned; he must be content as a sinner to find the Saviour. And here fatal pride prevails to the ruin of how many souls! It is what makes the Lord insist so strongly upon the necessity of repentance, for repentance is just this bringing down of creature-pride to receive, as needing it, God's salvation. The "ninety and nine just persons" of whom He speaks in the parable "need no repentance": the figure of a repentant sinner is a "sheep that was lost." Such lost ones the tender grace of Christ goes after "till He finds." Confessedly lost sinners now, they are finally *never* lost. On the other hand, even His lips must say, "Except ye repent, ye shall all likewise perish."

Now, if we come back to Samaria, and God's bestowal of His blessing there, we can easily see how God's announcement comes in most suited order just where it does. The king stands here, as ever in Israel, as the representative of the equally guilty people. And this king, the wicked descendant of as wicked ancestors, awakened to his danger, although not his sin, had put on the garb of repentance,— Job's sackcloth without Job's self-abhorrence. He talks piously of the Lord: "If the Lord do not help thee, whence shall I help thee?" And all this not as hypocrisy,— the sackcloth is not outside for the people to see, but "within, upon his flesh." He is seeking to establish a claim upon God by that which is the sign that he has *no* claim. And how many, not in the least hypocrites, are doing that! They will turn their repentance itself into a kind of righteousness, when the very meaning of repentance is that we have none. And God waits, and defers the blessing which it is in His heart to give, because if He gave it, He would be putting His sanction upon what is quite untrue. The king's sackcloth was, in this way, the very hindrance to blessing. To have given it before this was stripped off would have been to have obscured His precious grace, and to have turned into wages His free gift. He delays, therefore, the blessing; lets the ungodliness of the king's heart come out; and then, when all pretension upon man's part is entirely excluded, brings in His grace as *grace*, without a stain upon its glory, to be a witness of the principles of His gospel to us to-day.

Blessed be His name! Every soul that has a true sense of sin will thank Him for it adoringly. Is there not some soul that listens to me now who will now accept for the first time this free and priceless grace,— not now a temporal but an eternal salvation? "Ho! every one that thirsteth, come ye to the waters; and he that hath no money, come ye, buy and eat! Yea, come, buy wine and milk without money and without price!"

But God has much more to speak of in this precious history, and still more will emphasize for us the riches of His grace. We have now to mark the way the blessing actually comes. For this purpose God takes up "four leprous men," outcasts even among the wretched inhabitants of the city, just as God took up once the chief of sinners, Saul of Tarsus, to preach the fullest, sweetest story of grace that has ever been published to the world. If the shadow of death had fallen on all the city, how must it have pressed upon these forlorn men! And it is out of their despair their hope arises. Who else would have found hope in going out to the camp of the Syrians? But for them death compassed them around; "and they said unto one another 'Why sit we here until we die? If we say, We will enter into the city, then the famine is in the city, and we shall die there; and if we sit still here, we die also. Now therefore come, and let us fall into the host of the Syrians: if they save us alive, we shall live; and if they kill us, we shall but die.'"

It was the very place and power of death for that besieged city, and out of it was to come that which would save alive Samaria's starving multitude. Out of the eater was to come meat; out of the strong, sweetness. And so for us also that riddle of Samson's must be fulfilled. For ourselves, our natural portion is death and judgment; and which of us has any ability to meet these? Death is the stamp of a ruined world; and if God enter into judgment with us, no flesh living shall be justified. Here is the stronghold of the enemy against us; and thus through fear of death men are all their lifetime subject to bondage. At a distance from it, although we know full well what awaits us, we may, with the incredible stolidity which belongs to man, think little perhaps about it. In Samaria for some time doubtless the dance and the song went on. Nay, even as the certain doom drew near, it may be there were those who only held more frantically to the revels that for the moment could still divert them from what they dared not contemplate.

A mighty work God had been doing for Samaria, but these we may be sure knew nothing of it. It pleased God to communicate the secret of what He had done to these four leprous men: "And they rose up in the twilight to go unto the camp of the Syrians; and when they were come to the uttermost part of the camp of Syria, behold, there was no man there. For the Lord had made the host of the Syrians to hear a noise of chariots, and a noise of horses, even the noise of a great host; and they said one to another, 'Lo, the king of Israel hath hired against us the kings of the Hittites and the kings of the Egyptians to come upon us.' Wherefore they arose and fled in the twilight, and left their tents, and their horses, and their asses, even the camp as it was, and fled for their life." God had worked alone, and no one with Him, needing no help, and for those wholly unable to give it. And thus for faith Christ has "abolished death, and brought life and incorruption to light through the gospel." "He has spoiled principalities and powers"; "has led captivity captive, and given gifts unto men." Alone He has done it. "Whither I go," He says to Peter, "thou canst not follow me now." But the work accomplished, we are welcome to share the fruits of His victory. They are as free to us as the camp of the Syrians to those four leprous men. Absolutely free it was: "They went into one tent, and did eat and drink, and carried thence silver and gold and raiment, and went and hid it; and came again, and entered into another tent, and carried thence also, and went and hid it." How sudden the change from the death that stared them in the face to this abundance! How surpassingly wonderful to him who finds himself reaping the spoil of death, the fruit of Christ's victory! It is all ours without reserve, nothing kept back, "silver and gold and raiment,"— things which have very plain significance in the word of God. Let us try and spell them out, and see what our riches are, although after all their value may no man tell.

It is not enough for God to deliver,— He must enrich also those whom He delivers. The deliverance, too, is, in the way of its accomplishment, infinite riches to us; and of this first the *silver* speaks. The atonement-money was silver, the witness to redemption, which for us "is not with silver and gold, but with the precious blood of Christ." Redemption is the testimony of what is in the heart of God toward us. If we needed the ransom, God has not thought even such a price too great. What infinite blessedness to find ourselves of this value to One to whom all worlds belong: "God so loved the world that He gave His only begotten Son." Prodigals, beggars, bankrupts, as we are, the whole of the universe does not equal the price that has been paid for us. We can tell our riches, then, in this, when what we have cost Him is the measure of the love which invites and welcomes us — the "love of Christ that passeth knowledge"!

And then the "gold": gold is divine glory, the outshining of what He is who is light, and now *in* the light. The darkness in which for the moment He was hidden who for us went into it is for faith past, and already the true light shines. Our inheritance is in the light. We know God,— are already worshipers in the holiest of all, — can worship in spirit and in truth,— for we know whom we worship.

What wealth is ours in this glory which streams out upon us,— in which we live,— which brightens all our path, glorifying even now all the clouds which hang over it,— which illuminates even such as we are to reflect it: "For God, who commanded the light to shine out of darkness, hath shined in our hearts, to give *out* the light of the glory of God in the face of Jesus Christ." It is thus we know Him,— in righteousness, in truth, in unfailing, everlasting love; and then the light of an eternal day has risen upon us, and a wealth beyond that of unnumbered worlds is in our hands.

"And raiment": for then, too, is the shame of our nakedness removed. We are clothed with that which not only completely covers us in the sight of God, but with the best robe even in the Father's house, for we are clothed with Christ Himself; we stand in Him, accepted in the Beloved, seen in the value of that priceless work which has maintained, in fully tried perfection, the character of God in the very place in which He suffered for the sins of men. We thus in Christ before God are made, not only the display of His grace, but of His righteousness also,—"made the righteousness of God in Him."

How sudden the change, I say again, for these poor lepers, from famine and destitution to this abundance verily theirs to lay hold of as they list! God had wrought alone for them, and they had but to enjoy the fruits; and that place of death had changed for them its character wholly,— it was the place of life, and peace, and marvelous riches. But it is only, after all, the feeble picture, however blessed, of what God has done for us. Beloved, is it, through God's grace, indeed our own? And if so, how far are we realizing our infinite possessions?

But a thought strikes them in the midst of their happiness; and while, after all, it is in them a selfish one, we shall do well to heed the lesson of it: "Then they said one to another, 'We do not well; this day is a day of good tidings, and we hold our peace: if we tarry till the morning light, some evil will come upon us: now therefore come, that we may tell it to the king's household.'"

If we have been able thus far to follow the interpretation of this, should it be needful to make the application here? Surely the need around should sufficiently appeal to those who by grace are partakers of an infinite treasure, which in sharing with others we only realize ourselves the more! Think of needing to be stirred up as to this! And yet we do need; and because of our lack in this respect, does not evil come upon us too under the holy government of God? If "he that withholdeth corn the people shall curse him," what is the responsibility of those who hold back from perishing souls the "word of life,"— the good word that can make glad the saddest heart,— yea, make the tongue of the dumb to sing for joy?

Back, then, they go to the city, and tell the well-nigh incredible story, none the less true. I pass over the reception of it,— the wisdom of the king which counts it but deceit,— the need of the people which forces to test if it be not true. God invites this experimental test, beloved friends. Christianity is a religion of experiment; and if only there be lowliness and need on the part of the seeker, he shall not be turned away.

But I pass on to just one final word, which we must not miss; for the Spirit of God emphasizes, by minute repetition of the sin which brought it down, the judgment of God upon the scorner of His precious grace. More solemn than any words which I could use are the words of the inspired historian to one who died in the very midst of the abundance which the prophet had predicted: "So a measure of fine flour was sold for a shekel, and two measures of barley for a shekel, according to the word of the Lord. And the king appointed the lord on whose hand he leaned to have charge of the gate; and the people trod upon him in the gate, and he died, as the man of God had said who spake when the king came down to him. And it came to pass as the man of God had spoken to the king, saying, 'Two measures of barley for a shekel, and a measure of fine flour for a shekel, shall be to-morrow about this time in the gate of Samaria.' And that lord answered the man of God, 'Now, behold, if the Lord should make windows in heaven, might this thing be?' And he said, 'Behold, thou shalt see it with thine eyes, but shalt not eat thereof.' And so it fell out unto him; for the people trod upon him in the gate, and he died."

Thank God for the blessed word which says "He that liveth and believeth on Me shall *never* die."

# THE LOST SHEEP.

(Luke xv. 1-7.)

NOT only are the *mines* of Scripture yet little worked, there is a wealth of precious things yet upon the surface which we have never made our own, for all the centuries we have had the fields in our possession. What are we more familiar with than the parables of this chapter? They are the constant theme of the evangelist; they are among the most prized treasures of faith everywhere. They are sung in hall and in street, lisped by childhood and studied by youth, and often link for the dying the most precious memories of the past with the joys into which they are entering. And yet, even among so-called evangelical Christians, how often do we find contradictory conceptions of these very parables! If we ask, Who are the "ninety and nine just persons who need no repentance"? who are the two "sons" of the last parable? how is it that the father says to the elder son, "All that I have is thine"? we shall find very different answers given by different persons of at least the average intelligence in spiritual things.

It is no purpose of mine to take up these differences, but rather to look at the parables themselves for what the Lord in His grace may grant us out of them for edification and blessing; only making the diversity of view the argument for closer examination of their meaning and design. One thing is sure: however often we may have come to these divine springs, we shall find still that there is fresh and living water. Blessed are they only that hunger and thirst: they shall ever be filled.

The occasion of the three parables was a common one and they are so manifestly linked together in subject, all the more clearly because of their individual differences, that scarcely a question can be raised on that score. In each case, what has been lost is found; in each, the joy —the basis, and the crowning joy—is, blessed be God, in the one who finds what he has lost. The threefold story of the love that seeks and finds suggests (what a further view confirms abundantly) that here it is the heart of the whole Godhead that is told out to us. Father, Son, and Spirit are all occupied with man. Around him revolves an interest that makes all things its witnesses, and servants for its blessed purposes.

The occasion is this, that there "were drawing near unto Him all the publicans and sinners for to hear Him." And the Pharisees and scribes murmured, saying, "This man receiveth sinners, and eateth with them."

Our common version says, "*Then* drew near," but the words do not speak of what merely happened at a certain time, but of what was habitually taking place. We see that everywhere through the gospels, from the day at least in which He called Levi from the receipt of custom, and Levi made Him a feast in his own house, "publicans and sinners" flocked around the Lord. They had gone out largely to John's baptism before that, when through the gate of repentance they were invited to come to find remission of their sins. Now, when grace sought them more openly, it was to be expected that they, beyond others, would welcome it. And they did. "Verily I say unto you," were Christ's words to the Pharisees, "that the publicans and harlots go into the kingdom of God before you. For John came unto you in the way of righteousness, and ye believed him not, but the publicans and the harlots believed him; and ye, when ye saw it, did not even repent yourselves afterward, that ye might believe him." (Matt. xxi. 31, 32.)

The Pharisees resented the grace that welcomed such; for this grace makes its own demand, and, with the inflexibility of law itself, will abate nothing. "Except ye repent, ye shall all likewise perish," is harshness indeed to "just persons who have no need of repentance;" and this is how the parable itself describes those to whom, as murmurers against His ways, He is replying. Surely it is evident that if in the last parable alone this murmuring is distinctly found in the person of the elder son, the first no less pictures the two parties to whom alike they were uttered.

People look around to find a class who have no need of repentance, and some who cannot find them on earth apply our Lord's words to the angels! A common hymn we sing speaks of the same class as—

> "The ninety and nine that safely lay
> In the shelter of the fold,"

but of this the parable says nothing. The mistake is in making a reality out of what is but the image in a mirror which the Lord puts before His audience that they may recognize themselves. And from this He necessarily pictures them according to their own estimate of themselves,—an estimate which He uses at the same time for the purpose of conviction on the one side, of encouragement on the other. *Had* he pictured them other than their own thought, the arrow would have missed its mark. How could they fail to apply aright these righteous men whom He exhibited to them in contrast with this wandering sheep,—"lost," or self-destroyed? How could they interpret wrongly this "elder son" serving his father in the field, indignantly pleading against the free reception of his unworthy brother his own ill-requited years of toil? Yet after all, in what seems to admit their fullest claim, they find themselves convicted and exposed, their argument refuted, and their heartlessness and distance from God laid bare.

Yet withal God Himself is at the same time so wondrously revealed, that when the scene closes with that direct appeal upon the father's part—"Then came his father out and entreated him,"—you listen involuntarily for the sudden sob which shall tell of another heart, no less a prodigal's, broken down into confession and return.

The scribes taught much in parables. The Lord will have them listen to parables in turn. We feel, in the style in which He addressses Himself to them here, that the reason is not that which He gives upon another occasion to His disciples: "Therefore speak I unto them in parables, because they seeing see not, and hearing they hear not, neither do they understand." No doubt, here as elsewhere, the parable would, like the seed of which He was speaking in the former case, test the receptive character of the ground upon which it fell. Yet the pleading in them cannot be mistaken either. Did He not, as just now said, Himself picture the Father as entreating even the Pharisee? Could He do less, or hide from them in words hard to be interpreted, that very entreaty?

The gentlest, most persuasive, winning form of speech is undoubtedly the parable. There is the attractiveness of the story itself, as the lips here could tell it, taking possession of one before even its meaning might become plain, and then detaining the soul to listen to that meaning. There is the hold upon the memory which we all realize, by virtue of which it might, like incorruptible seed, lodge in the frozen ground until a more genial time should give it leave to expand and root itself. With how many has it not been so since! and how great a harvest may we not be sure will yet be seen to have sprung from this sowing! Sow it in some hearts afresh even now, blest Sower, Son of Man, for Thy love's sake!

"What man of you, having a hundred sheep, if he lose one of them, doth not leave the ninety and nine in the wilderness, and go after that which is lost, until he find it?

"And when he hath found it, he layeth it on his shoulders rejoicing.

"And when he cometh home, he calleth together his friends and neighbors, saying unto them, Rejoice with me, for I have found my sheep which was lost.

"I say unto you that likewise joy shall be in heaven over one sinner that repenteth, more than over ninety and nine just persons which need no repentance."

They have assailed Him for His love, and the Lord first of all, therefore, answers for Himself. He will afterward, though in a more covert way, show how the Spirit, and then openly how the Father, is of one mind with Him. Are *they* not too? He asks. If it were only a sheep that was in question, there would be no doubt. Alas, that doubt could only come in where *men* were concerned! Would they indeed value a man lower than a sheep? But these were His: put them upon that low level, who should forbid His interest in them?

He does not compare Himself to the shepherd here. He might act as that, but He was much more than that —even the Owner of the sheep. We see that he makes the loftiest claim here. They are *His*,—even these poor publicans and sinners. He who made and fashioned them is He who is in pursuit of them. Will they question His right?

It is a first principle for faith that God is the seeker; that there is heart in Him,—goodness in Him. We are not bid to batter at closed doors. We have not to soften Him to pity, or turn Him toward us. We feel our hardness toward Him, and we think Him hard. We listen to our consciences that accuse us, and we think we hear His voice in them, who yet "upbraideth not." What a revelation of God is this, when Christ, down here among men, becomes His true and only representative!

Conscience is *not* the voice of God to us. It is the voice of self-conviction, of the moral nature within us, pronouncing upon ourselves, and which makes us rightly anticipate a judgment to come. But even here, while it is the eye to see, there is no less required the light to see. In the twilight darkness in which so many are shrouded, what is unreal is oftentimes confounded with the real. If a poor Romanist omits his worship of the Virgin, conscience may smite him for it. If he gets his absolution from the priest, he feels relieved and happy. Of many, Scripture says, "Even their mind and *conscience* is defiled." (Tit. i. 15.) It may have its fools' paradise or its fabled purgatory. As the light comes in, reality succeeds to the unreal, and in the day that comes there will be nothing hid.

But conscience can never take the place of revelation. God only can tell me what He is, or what Christ did for me, or how my soul can be at peace with Him. For all this, I must listen to the Word alone. It alone can bring in the true eternal light in which conscience and heart alike can find their rest and satisfaction forever.

God reveals Himself then as Seeker. It is He whose the sheep are who is come after them. In this character

He is for the lost, the wandered, though it be, as with these publicans, that worst wandering, heart and mind astray, and astray hopelessly, without power of self-recovery. A bottomless word, this "lost"! Not even the Pharisees would have uttered it of these publicans; for they believed in an inherent power in man by which, though by painful effort and perseverance, the crooked might be straightened yet. Were there not legal sacrifices and prescribed restitutions, ablutions, and purifications?

Divine love saw *lost* ones,—saw in its full extent the misery which it alone was adequate to relieve, and that misery, so hopeless otherwise, brought it down on their behalf. The Creator becomes the Saviour. He "goeth after that which is lost until He find it." With the divine power and wisdom in pursuit, there is no uncertainty here as to success. Help is laid upon One who is mighty, with whom to fail would be indeed irretrievable disaster, convulsing heaven and earth in universal ruin. But there is no fear: the cause of the helpless is become the cause of the Almighty, "to the praise of the glory of His grace."

Pharisees, publicans, and sinners alike knew who were these lost ones, thus made the objects of God's special interest. No one of them needed to inquire, as so many to-day are found inquiring, "Is this for me?" It was a definite gospel addressing itself without any possibility of question to those whose hearts claimed so great salvation, and whose consciences put them in this strangely privileged class. They had but to take the divine estimate of them to find themselves enrolled among the heirs of salvation. And here, marvelous to say, communion with God begins for the poor sinner who thus is at one with God as to his condition and his need.

**Light has shone in upon the soul, and though it be but**

upon ruin, yet here also, as in the six days' work, God sees the light that it is good. It is the proof of a work begun which shall end only in the rest of God when at last *all* is good. The soul is in His presence whose presence yet shall be fullness of joy to it. We are *new*-born, as born naturally, with a cry.

"Until He find it." He has made the responsibility of that His own. Blest news for the consciously helpless, —the work is His. The effect of this sweet assurance, where it takes hold, is that Christ is revealed in it. The lost *are* found: the everlasting arms are realized to be about them. Not more surely are they disclosed to themselves than He is disclosed to them. This is rest begun. He has given it.

"He goeth after that which is lost until He find it." Then these lost are found. Infinite power and love are on the track and cannot fail. It is plain, then, that the Lord is speaking, not of all men as in a lost condition (for all men are *not* found), but for the ear and heart of these who were flocking now around Him. His words are no mere generalities, powerless to minister to the need of souls, but divine seed finding its own place, and rooting itself in the furrows of the plowed-up ground, where the work of the Spirit gives it entrance.

It is a blessed thing to be able to give a free and general offer of salvation,—to say, "Christ died for all: come to Him, and He will give you rest." Yet there are those who need even a closer individualization. There are those who lie wounded by the road-side, needing, not merely the call of the gospel, but the grasp of the strong, tender hands, and the binding up of the gaping wounds. There are those to whom, if they cannot appropriate Him, Christ would appropriate Himself,—those who dare not thrust out leprous hands to Him because of their pollution, and who can only be liberated and brought out of their isolation by that direct touch of His, in which a new, undreamed-of life for them begins.

"He goeth after that which is lost." How much do those quiet words involve!

> "But none of the ransomed ever knew
>   How deep were the waters crossed;
> Nor how dark was the night which the Lord passed through,
>   Ere He found His sheep which was lost."

The cross was the only place in which He could overtake these wanderers. It is only as we realize what the cross is, that we find the arms of this mighty love thrown round us. Here indeed He has come where we are. Here is the place in which, without rebuke, we can claim Him, —*our* place, the place of our doom,—our substitute and sin-bearer He who takes it. The awful cloud which has shadowed His glory has destroyed forever the distance between us. The crucified One is ours; for the death and judgment He has borne are ours. These are our due,—our penalty; and we have them in the cross borne, and borne away from us. He has found the lost; and immediately we are freed and upborne by the might of this redemption and by the living power of the Redeemer: "He layeth it upon His shoulders rejoicing."

How blessed is this! What *can* be the force of such words, but to assure us of the complete triumph of divine love in the poor sinner's salvation! There is to be no trusting him to himself again; no possible forfeiture of all the toil and pains of divine love in his behalf. The joy is His who brings back His own. The loss now would be indeed *His* loss. The failure clearly, as represented here, would be His. Failure, then, there cannot be. Put all the weakness, folly, waywardness of the now recovered one in the strongest way, and prove them by the most conclusive of arguments, what does all this do but furnish the most satisfactory reason *why the sheep should be where it is*, upon the shoulders of the shepherd, and not upon its own feet?

This, then, is salvation in the Lord's thought of it in this parable. It is salvation "to the uttermost" (Heb. vii. 25),—complete, eternal (chap. v. 9) salvation. This alone suits the case; alone gives peace to the conscience, alone gives rest to the heart. And it is here assured to every one who, looking to the Saviour, finds himself in this company of lost ones, after whom is His special quest. And how beautifully, in this freest of gospels, is repentance thus insisted on as inseparable from saving faith! "And when he cometh home, he calleth together his friends and his neighbors, saying unto them, 'Rejoice with me, for I have found my sheep which was lost.' I say unto you that likewise joy shall be in heaven over one sinner that repenteth, more than over ninety and nine just persons, which need no repentance."

Here the moral is plainly reached, and the application is easy. Who is the sinner that repenteth? Beyond all possible doubt, the sheep which was lost. Who are the just persons that need no repentance? As plainly, those who have never been thus consciously and hopelessly astray. It is to the *consciousness* of those before Him the Lord appeals; and upon this depends the force of that appeal. These publicans and sinners who as such flocked to hear the message of grace, were those in whom was repentance; and so the gospel, with all its real freedom *selects* (so to speak) its recipients. The ninety and nine just persons who need no repentance have, on this very account, no need of and no taste for *grace*. No less certainly than the needle follows the magnet do these convicted sinners follow and cleave to Christ.

There are many teachers,—there are many and conflicting teachings,—there were at that time, there have been ever; yet we are not left to this confusion and uncertainty. Nor are the simplest and most ignorant left to be the dupes of those subtler than themselves. No, there is a rule of God's moral goverment which forbids such a result. For, let a man but face his own convictions,—let him only admit the sin which his conscience, if not hardened, witnesses against him, and realize the helplessness which soon discovers itself to those in earnest to be delivered, —there is but one voice that can be authoritative for him any more. The jangle of contending voices is hushed; scribes, doctors of the law, names, and parties, and schools of thought become utterly insignificant. Faith hears only Him who says, with calmness and assurance, "Come unto ME, and I will give you rest."

It is the Lord; and He who invites to rest, Himself rests in the rest He gives. It is that for which He has labored. "Sing, O daughter of Zion; shout, O Israel . . . the Lord thy God in the midst of thee is mighty: He will save; He will rejoice over thee with joy; He will rest in His love; He will joy over thee with singing." (Zeph. iii. 17.)

# THE LOST PIECE OF SILVER.

(Luke xv. 8–10.)

THE second parable of this chapter, brief as it is, is undoubtedly the most difficult of the three, and that not merely because of its brevity. The thought of the woman, and that of the house, seem to introduce elements which if intelligible from a Christian are all the less so from a Jewish stand-point. Yet we may not omit them as of no importance. Scripture is nowhere less than perfect, and to impute what is our own ignorance to defect in it is irreverent folly. Let us see, then, what light may be gained by patient examination of the parable in dependence upon Him who alone can teach effectually.

It is certain that in all the three the joy of *recovery* is set before us,—the joy, blessed to hear of, in the *presence of* the angels—divine joy in the fullest sense. In the first parable, it is that of the Shepherd—of Christ Himself; in the last, it is the Father's joy who receives,—yet not only receives, for the son is yet "a long way off" when He sees and has compassion, and runs, and falls upon his neck, and kisses him. The second parable must give us, then, one would say, the joy of the Spirit, and thus the whole heart of God be manifested to us.

The central figure here — that of a woman—at first sight may present a difficulty. A woman might well be a

picture of the Church of God,—of the saints of God,—
and such we have elsewhere in the Word. But then these
thoughts are after all not so far asunder. The Spirit of
God works through the Word; the Word is carried by the
saints; thus indirectly He may be represented in what is
directly their picture. And how else, indeed, one may
ask, could He be more fitly? While most graciously thus
redeemed sinners are not only themselves joyed over, but
taken in to share the joy of heaven also over the salvation
of others.

Thus the "woman" seems intelligible, and the figure
of wisdom in the book of Proverbs may remind us that
after all it is not altogether foreign to the Old Testament
Scriptures. Here, as we might expect in the gospels, the
object of her search is more helpless, more absolutely
dependent upon the love that goes out after it; and this
does not in the least affect the suitability of the story
here. Rather is it all in divine harmony.

So is it in keeping that we hear now of a lamp lighted
for the search,—the figure, of course, of the Word of God
as lighted amid the darkness of the world. Yet the Spirit
of God must light it up if it is to manifest where the lost
soul is,—often in corners dark and secret enough, and
sadly covered with dust and smut of sin, so that you would
not recognize it at all as having the value that it has for
God. A lost piece of silver speaks of this value; a lost
*soul* may easily overbalance the whole world gained.
The atonement-money in Israel was paid in silver; and
atonement it is that exhibits the true value of a soul
gained for God—*re*gained, for He all through is the owner
of it. "Behold, all souls are Mine," He says. Ah, what
diligent search would we not make if we thought of the
stamp of the royal mint upon the lowest and most de-
graded among men, and saw the value of souls with God

in the price paid for them—saw the sheen of silver glitter in the lamplight out of the dust of some neglected corner!

We must sweep the house! But the dust will fly, and this sweeping is not a pleasant occupation. To make a stir about sin is unpleasant enough, no doubt, but the broom turns, if it be a little roughly sometimes, the king's money out of its hiding-place.

The house must be swept. It is the place of natural ties and relationships—those links by which God would bring us together and make us objects of interest to one another. It is within this circle that we shall find most profit in sweeping—most readily come across the precious coins for God's treasury. Many are ready to do street-sweeping, and testify abroad for Christ, who have no heart for it in the familiar circles in which after all are the nearest and most recompensing fields of labor. The witness of the home, of the place of business, of the familiar and accustomed life, is the most fruitful—the God-ordained first place at least of labor, which if we occupy, we may be promoted, but not else. Ah, if we would sweep the house!—nothing so marks the work of the Holy Ghost as this, in which the good work will be measured, however, not by the amount of dust that is raised, but by the pieces of silver that we find. For if "he that winneth souls is wise," he that is wise, too, shall win them. This close and homely work God blesses: the house is cleansed by it; but more, that which has been lost is found. Oh, be sure, this woman at her housework may read us a true gospel-lesson, and every woman at her housework may thus have the joy of the evangelist, and the labor of love that fails not; for love's labor is never lost.

What characterizes the day is so much official evangelism, with so little simple natural testimony according to the apostolic order—"I believed, and therefore have I spoken:" the necessary outflow of full hearts, of those that have been in Christ's company, and cannot forbear to say to those around what it costs no education, no special gift, to say,—"Come, see a Man which told me all things that ever I did; is not this the Christ?" A great and effectual preacher was that poor Samaritan woman! What had made her so? What she says herself,—the company of Christ. Christ had been speaking to her. It is this that looses the tongue and gives it eloquence indeed.

Is it not striking that when the Lord would give us here the share which His people can have in the joy of heaven, that He gives us, not a crier in the market-place, but this quiet and unseen toiler in the house. "It is only an illustration," some will say. Well, it is an illustration out of which the thoughtful and the humble will get help and courage, and thank Him for it. Let the crier cry too in the market-place, and thank God for that! But if it were a choice between the two (which it is not), better would it be to have the necessary testimony of faith—"I believed, and therefore I have spoken,"—in every private Christian than the more public testimony even. Could we have this aright, how would the Old Testament scripture be fulfilled, "The Lord gave the Word: great was the company of those that published it"—as the words imply, the *"women"* that published it." (Ps. lxviii. 11.) *This* woman-preaching would indeed be effectual work.

The joy is here as in the other parables: "And when she hath found it, she calleth her friends and her neighbors together, saying, 'Rejoice with me, for I have found the piece which I had lost.' Likewise, I say unto you, there is joy in the presence of the angels of God over one sinner that repenteth."

And the joy of the Holy Ghost, will He not make it

felt in the hearts of His people? "Friends" He must have with whom to share it. It is diffusive, multiplying itself as it travels from heart to heart, as a fire increases with fresh fuel. Such shall be the joy of eternity,—the joy of one the joy of all,—the pervasive joy of love, than which there is nothing sweeter, nothing purer, nothing higher. It is indeed the joy of God Himself, for "God is love."

# THE LOST SON.

(Luke xv. 11-24.)

THE third parable of this chapter, while it reveals no less than the former ones the heart of God, reveals on the other hand, more than these, the heart of man, and that whether as receiving or rejecting the grace that seeks him. It is in this respect the fitting close of the appeal to conscience. Publican and Pharisee are both shown fully to themselves in the holy light which yet invites and welcomes all who will receive it.

Whatever applications may be made to Jew and Gentile, it should be plain that these are but applications, however legitimate, and that the Lord is not addressing Himself to a class outside His present audience, but to the practical need of those before Him. The same consideration decisively forbids the thought of any direct reference to the restoration of a child of God gone astray from Him, an interpretation which makes of the elder son who had not wandered the pattern saint! Strange it is indeed that any who know what the grace of God does in the soul of its recipient should ever entertain so strange a notion. It is one of the fruits of reading Scripture apart from its context, as if it were a mosaic of disconnected fragments: a thing, alas! still done by so many, to the injury of their souls. We hope to look at the elder son at another time, but the foundation of this strange view meets us at the outset.

The two who are in evident contrast throughout here are both called "sons." And so in the first parable are the ninety and nine, as well as the object of the Shepherd's quest called "sheep." But we know the Jewish fold held other flocks than those of Christ in it. When He enters it, He calleth His own sheep by name, and leadeth them out. (Jno. x. 3.) The fact, then, of all being called sheep need perplex no one.

The title of "son" may indeed seem to involve more than this, because Judaism taught no "Abba, Father," and it is one of the characteristics of Christianity that we receive in it "the adoption of sons." While this is true, it is by no means the whole truth. Israel too had an "adoption" (Rom. ix. 3); and it is with reference to their position in contrast with the Gentiles that the Lord said to the Syro-phenician woman, "It is not meet to take the *children's* bread, and to cast it unto the dogs." In the parable, the Lord spoke to the Jews after His solemn entry into Jerusalem; He again speaks of both Pharisees and publicans, joining "harlots" with the latter as sons, precisely as here,—"A certain man had *two sons*." (Matt. xxi. 28.) Thus, while the proper truth of relationship to God could only be known and enjoyed in Christianity, it is certain that Israel had also, as the only one of the families of the earth "known" to Him, a place upon which they valued themselves, and it was just that generation among whom the Lord stood, who did above all claim this. "We be not born of fornication" was their indignant reply to Him upon another occasion, "we have one Father, even God." (Jno. viii. 41.) And though He urges upon them the want of real correspondence in their character, yet there was basis sufficient for His utterance here, while the want of correspondence comes out in the end too as fully. "I am a Father to Israel" had long since been declared.

The character of the younger son soon becomes manifest. "Give me the portion of goods that falleth to me" is itself significant. He is not content that his father should keep his portion, but will have it to enjoy, himself, in independence of the hand from which it comes. You do not wonder to learn that in a little while he would be freer still, and that the far country is for him an escape from his father's eye, as the independent portion had been from his hand.

It need hardly be said that this is the way in which men treat God. That which comes from Him, the Author of all the good in it for which they seem to have so keen a relish, such entire appreciation, they yet cannot enjoy in submission to Him or in His presence. God is their mar-all—the destruction of all their comfort. How many "inventions" have they to forget Him! for the "far-off country" is itself but one of these. God is "*not far off* from any one of us." Oh, what a desolation would these very children of disobedience find it, if indeed they could banish God from His own world!

It is no wonder that in this far-off country the prodigal should waste his substance with riotous living. It is only the sign that where he is is beginning to tell on him; the touch of coming famine is already on him. The little good in any thing apart from God felt by one still not in the secret of it makes him hunt after it the more; and if there be only a pound of sugar in a ton of sap, the sap will go very quickly in finding the sugar. This is what the man is doing,—going in the company of the "many who say, 'Who will show us any good?'" and who have not learned to say, "Lord, lift Thou up the light of Thy countenance upon us."

So the wheels run fast down-hill. Soon he is at the bottom. He has spent all, and *then* there arises a mighty famine in the land. It is not only that his own resources are at an end, but the whole land of his choice is stripped and empty. This is fulfilled with us when we have not merely lost what was our own, but have come to find that in all the world there is nothing from which to supply ourselves. It is not an experience—perhaps an exceptional experience—of our own, but the cry of want is every where. How can we even *beg* from *beggars?* Such is the world when the eye is opened really as to it,—when the ear has come to interpret its multitudinous sounds. Every where are leanness and poverty. Every where is the note of the passing bell. "The world passeth away, and the lust thereof."

Then he goes and joins himself to a citizen of that far-off land,—one who belongs to it as, according to this story, even the prodigal did not. For men have come into this condition, but are not looked upon as hopelessly involved in it. There is elsewhere a Father's heart that travels after them: there is the step of One who goeth after that which is lost. But the citizen of that far-off land has no ties,—not even (one may say) *broken* ties elsewhere. Such a citizen the devil assuredly is, and the troop he is feeding and fattening for destruction speak plainly for him: "*he* sent him into his fields to feed *swine.*"

These swine, alas! are *men*, —not all men, not even all natural men. They are those before whom the Lord forbids to cast the pearls of holy things, for they will trample them under their feet, and turn upon and rend you. They are the scoffers and scorners, the impious opposers of all that is of God. These are the company the devil entertains and feeds,—though with "husks,"—and indeed it must be owned he has no better provisions. These "husks," whatever they may be naturally, are surely *spiritually* just what would be food to profanity and impiety. The world's famine does not diminish Satan's resources in this respect,—nay, they are in some sense increased by it. All the misery of man, the fruit of his sin, the mark of divine judgment upon it, but also the warning voice of God by which He would emphasize His first question to the fallen, "Adam, where art thou?"—all this is what profanity would cast up against God. God, not man, it says, is the sinner; and man, not God, will be justified in judgment!

But the swine are swine evidently, rooting in the mire, men in their swinish grovelings and lusts that drive them; and those that feed them cannot after all fill their belly with that which the swine eat. For those who cannot always look down and willingly ignore what is above them, even though storms sweep through it as well as sunshine floats through it, cannot be satisfied with what, in leveling them with the beasts, degrades them below them. The beasts may be—*are* satisfied. They look not at death, and have no instincts which lead them beyond it: *they* may be satisfied "to lie in cold obstruction and to rot;" man never really. And it is more than questionable if, with all his powers of self-deception, he can ever quite believe it is his portion.

"And no man gave him." What is there like a land of famine for drying up all the sweet charities and affections that are yet left in men? Take the awful picture that Jeremiah gives, where "the hands of pitiful women have sodden their own offspring," as a sample of what this can do. And the estimate of men as beasts, the giving up of God and of the future life, does it tend to produce the pity of men for men? Have hospitals and asylums and refuges, and all the kindly ministrations of life, grown out of infidelity, or faith? Every one knows. The charity of the infidel seldom consists in more than freeing men from the restraints of conscience and the fear of God.

But here the prodigal "comes to himself." His abject misery stares him in the face. "Adam, where art thou?" is heard in his inmost soul; and if there be uncertainty as to all other things, here at least there is none. He is perishing with hunger. Not that he knows himself rightly yet, still less that he knows his father; but he is destitute, and there is bread in his father's house: he will arise and go to his father; he will say to him, "Father, I have sinned against heaven and before thee, and am no more worthy to be called thy son: make me as one of thy hired servants."

This is another point of which even the infidel may assure himself, that while he is starving, the people of God have real satisfaction and enjoyment. There need be no doubt about that. If it be a delusion that they enjoy, *yet they enjoy it*: if it be a falsehood that satisfies them, *yet they are satisfied*. And then it is surely strange that truth must needs make miserable, when a lie can satisfy! Nay, that Christ spake truth in this at least, that He said He would to those who came to Him give rest: and *He gives it*. Bolder in such a promise than any other ever dared to be, He yet *fulfills* His promise. While philosophy destroys philosophy, and schools of thought chase one another like shadows over the dial-plate of history, Christ's sweet assuring word never fails in fulfillment. Explain it as you may, you cannot deny it. Between His people and the world there is in this as clear a distinction as existed in Egypt when the three days' darkness rested on the land, "but all the children of Israel had light in their dwellings."

So the prodigal turns at last toward the light. There

is bread in his father's house. He will return. Yet he makes a great mistake. He says, "How many *hired servants* of my father's have bread enough and to spare!" And there is not even *one* hired servant in his father's house! God may "hire" a man of the world to do His will, just as He gave Egypt into the hand of Nebuchadnezzar as the "hire" for His judgment which he had executed upon Tyre. But in His *house* He has but children at His table: as it was said of the passover-feast, the type of it, "A foreigner and a *hired servant* shall not eat thereof." (Ex. xii. 45.)

He too—far off as he surely is yet—would come for his hire. He knows nothing as yet of the father's heart going out after him. He wrongs him with the very plea with which he intends to come, though it is indeed true that he is unworthy to be called his son. But this confession, in what different circumstances in fact does he make it!

"And he arose, and came to his father." Here is the great decisive point. Whatever may be the motives that influence him,—however little any thing yet may be right with him,—still he comes! And so the Lord presses upon every troubled weary soul to "come." However many the exercises of soul through which we pass, nothing profits till we come to Him. However little right anything may be with us beside, nothing can hinder our reception if we come. Him that cometh unto Him He will in no wise cast out.

So helpless we may be that we can come but in a look —"*Look* unto Me, and be ye saved, all the ends of the earth." Not "Look *at* Me" merely: men may look *at* Christ, and look long, and look with a certain kind of belief also, and look admiringly, and find no salvation in all this; but when Christ is the need—the absolute need, and the death-stricken soul pours itself out at the eyes to find the Saviour, though clouds and darkness may seem round about Him, yet shall it pierce through all. This is "coming." It is the might of weakness laying hold upon almighty strength. It is the constraint of need upon All-sufficiency. It is the power of misery over divine compassion. It is more than this: it is the Father's heart revealed.

For, "when he was yet a long way off, his father saw him, and had compassion, and ran, and fell on his neck, and kissed him." How it speaks of the way in which the father's heart had retained his image that he could recognize him in the distance, returning in such a different manner from that in which he had set out. Watching for him too, as it would seem; and when he saw him, forgetting all but that this was his son returned, in the impetuosity of irresistible affection, as if he might escape him yet, and he must secure him and hold him fast, running, and, in a love too great for words, falling upon his neck and making himself over to him in that passionate kiss! It is GOD of whom this is the picture! What a surprise for this poor prodigal! What an overwhelming joy for those who are met thus, caught in the arms of unchanging, everlasting love,—held fast to the bosom of God, to be His forever!

Not a question! not a condition! a word of it would have spoiled all. Holiness must be produced in us, not enforced, not bargained for. Tell this father upon his son's neck, if you can, that he is indifferent whether his son is to be his son or not. He who has come out in Christ to meet us, Friend of publicans and sinners, calls us to repentance by calling us to *Himself:* is there another way? "We joy in God through our Lord Jesus Christ, by whom we have now received the reconciliation." Is not this "joy in God" the sign of a heart brought back? of the far country, with all its ways, left forever behind?

*Christ is the kiss of God:* who that has received it has not been transformed by it? Who that, with the apostle John, has laid his head and his heart to rest upon His bosom, but with him will say, "He that sinneth hath not seen Him, neither known Him" (1 Jno. iii. 6)? That glorious vision—"the glory of that light"—blinded another apostle, not for three days only, but forever, to all other glory. "The life which I live in the flesh," he says, "I live by the faith of the Son of God, who loved me, and gave Himself for me." (Gal. ii. 20.)

Not until upon his father's bosom is the newly recovered one able to get out his meditated confession. Then in what a different spirit would it be made! The shameful "make me as one of thy hired servants" drops entirely out, while the sense of unworthiness deepens into true penitence. "The *goodness* of God" it is that "leadeth to repentance." The prompt reception, the sweet decisive assurance of the gospel, the "perfect love" that "casteth out fear,"—these are the sanctifying power of Christianity, its irresistible appeal to heart and conscience. Let no one dread the grace which alone liberates from the dominion of sin! If we have not known its power, it must be that we have not known itself. If we have found it feeble, it is only because we have feebly realized it. There is nothing beside it worthy to be trusted,—nothing that can be substituted for it, nothing that can supplement it or make it efficacious. The soul that cannot be purged by grace can only be subdued by the flames of hell!

The son may rightly confess his unworthiness, but the father cannot repent of his love: "But the father said to his servants, 'Bring forth the best robe, and put it on

him, and put a ring on his hand, and shoes on his feet.'"
He must be put into condition for the house he is coming into; but more, he must have the *best* robe in the house. And this, we know, is Christ. Christ must cover us from head to foot. Christ must cover us back and front. There must be no possible way of viewing us apart from Him. He it is who appears in the presence of God for us. Our Substitute upon the cross is our Representative in heaven. We are *in* Him,—"accepted in the Beloved." There can be no question at all that this is the best robe in heaven. No angel can say, Christ is my righteousness: the feeblest of the saved can say nothing else! It is Christ or self, and therefore Christ or damnation.

Oh, to realize the joy of this utter displacement of self by Christ! To accept it unreservedly is what will put us practically where the apostle was, and the things that were gain to *us* we count loss for Christ. Our possession in Him will become His possession of us, and there will be no separate interests whatever. How God has insured that our acceptance of our position shall set us right as to condition—make us His as He is ours! Here again too, how holy is God's grace! We are sanctified by that which justifies us; and the faith which puts us among the justified ones is the principle of all fruitfulness as well. The faith that has not works is thus dead: that is, it is no real faith at all.

Work is thus ennobled, and this I think you see in the "ring." The hand is thus provided for, and brought into corresponding honor with all the rest. What an honor to have a hand to serve Christ with! So the ring weds it to Him forever. We are no longer to serve ourselves. We are no longer to feed swine with husks. We are "made free from sin, and become servants to God; we have our fruit unto holiness, and the end everlasting life."

The person clothed, the hand consecrated, the feet are next provided for. The shoes are to enable us for the roughness of the way: and the apostle bids us have our feet shod with the "preparation of the gospel of peace." (Eph. vi. 15.) For the peace of the gospel is to apply itself to all the circumstances of the way. Our Father is the Lord of heaven and earth. Our Saviour sits upon the Father's throne. What enduring peace is thus provided for us! And as the shoe would arm against the defilement of the way, so it would be a guard against the dust and defilement of it. Can anything better prevent us getting under the power of circumstances (and so necessarily being defiled by them) than the quiet assurance that our God and Father holds them in His hand? To be ruffled and disturbed by them is to be thrown off our balance. We try our own methods of righting things, and our methods become less scrupulous as unbelief prevails with us: "Whatsoever is not of faith is sin." It is clear independency,—our will, not God's

Thus is the prodigal furnished! Again I say, how *holy* in its tender thoughtfulness is all this care! Blessed, blessed be God, *grace* is our sufficiency,—that is, Himself is. He is fully ours: we too—at least in the desire of our hearts—are fully His. And now the joy of eternity begins for us—communion in the Father's love. He is in heaven, we are on earth: in heaven the joy is; but we too are made sharers of it. Do we *not* share in what is here before us, "and bring hither the fatted calf, and kill it, and let us eat and be merry: for this my son was dead and is alive again; he was lost, and is found"?

It is the Father's joy, and over *us;* but Christ is the expression of it, and the One who furnishes the materials of it. The well-known figure of God's patient and fruitful Worker is before us, and the necessity, even for Him, of death, that we might live. God has wrought these things into our daily lives that we may continually have before us what is ever before Himself. And we are called to make Christ our own—to appropriate Him in faith in this intimate way, that as we abide in Him, He may abide in us. How He would assure us of our welcome to Him! How He would tell us that we are never to be parted! The life so ministered to, so sustained, is already within us the *eternal* life.

And the Father's joy fills the house, making all there to share it and to echo it. No impassive God is ours. The Author of this gushing spring of human feeling *no less* feels. We are in this also His offspring. "This my son was dead, and is alive again; he was lost, and is found." So the music and the dance begin, and shall never end.

# NOT LOST AND NOT SAVED.

## THE ELDER SON.

(Luke xv. 25-32.)

EVERY one of the class that were now following the Lord would realize in the prodigal his picture, and thus would find the invitation of grace superscribed with his name. Publicans and sinners would have the mirror plainly before them, and the truth in the description was absolute truth,—the condition of all men, if they could but realize it. With the other class who murmured against this grace, their lack of realization made it necessary to deal differently. *They* needed, above all, the mirror; and to be that, it must reflect the truth: but there would be a great difference in this respect, that the truth it conveyed would be no longer absolute, but only *relative* truth. Christ's words must exhibit them to themselves in such a way as they could *recognize* themselves; not, therefore, simply as God saw them, but according to their own thoughts about themselves; and yet with that in it which—appealing to their conscious experience—would bring them into the reality of what they were before God.

This is the whole difficulty as to the elder son in the last of our Lord's three parables here; and it is a difficulty which has already faced us in the first of them. The ninety and nine sheep which went not astray,—the ninety and nine just persons who need no repentance,—have no *real* representatives among men: yet they vividly portrayed those scribes and Pharisees who were *not* lost, and needed no Saviour. The light is let in there where it is said that there is more joy in heaven over one sinner that repenteth than over them.

In this last parable, the inner workings of the heart are much more exposed, and consequently these features of the first one are found in more development. But the whole is so plain that certainly the Pharisees here would make no mistake about the application. *They*, at least, would not think of Jews and Gentiles being in question, or of the recovery of a backslider: they would not think of the Lord meaning the whole lesson for others than themselves!

But there is nothing that is not clear if only we are at the right point of view. Thus that it is the *elder* son that represents the Pharisees has point in this way. Certainly they would not have accepted the position of the younger. To the elder belonged the birthright, with its double portion, in every way of value in the eyes of a Jew. On the other hand, in the book of Genesis, nothing is more distinct than the way the first-born all through *loses* the birthright. "That which is first is natural" merely, rings through the book. And even so it is here.

When the younger son is restored to his father's house, the elder son is in the field. It is characteristic of him that he is a worker, and a hard worker. All that is due is credited to the busy religion of the Pharisee. But his secret soon comes out: when he hears music and dancing in his father's house, he does not know what to make of it. It is not that he has heard yet of the return of his brother. It is not that he is simply a stranger to grace. But the sounds *in themselves* are unaccustomed ones: "he called a servant, and asked what these things meant." He is the picture of that joyless, cheerless service which finds nothing in God.  No pleasures are known as at His right hand forevermore.  The soul cannot say, "In Thy presence is fullness of joy."  There is work of a certain kind perhaps in plenty, but it is work in the field simply —afar off.  Such work is no test of piety; it is only the "work of *faith* and the labor of *love*" which are so.  And where faith and love are, the soul works amid music, and is never outside the Father's presence.  As His grace can be no surprise, so the merry heart sings with melody to the Lord,—"music and dancing" cannot surprise it.  Joy is the atmosphere in which we are called to live,—the strength for labor, the secret of holiness.  It can lodge in our hearts with sorrow, and abide all the changes of the way.  The apostle says, "He that sinneth hath not seen [Christ], neither known Him."  May we not say, "He that rejoiceth not, cannot have seen Christ"?

These Pharisees had Him before their eyes, yet saw Him not,—looked into His face, and knew Him not. Theirs was work in the field, while the Father's house was dull and pleasureless.  Thus to have it opened after this sort to publicans and sinners could not but anger them—could not but rouse an unwelcome voice in them —a voice they could not but hear, while they would not listen to it.  The truth commends itself to men's consciences, when their hearts reject it, hardened through a pride which will not brook humiliation.  Did the grace which showed itself so readily to other men refuse them? Nay, the gospel expressly comes out to all,—to every creature—in the same tender tones, addressing itself to all.  This elder brother had no door closed in his face. "He was angry, and would not go in."  Nor was there any thing of indifference toward him, but the contrary: "then came his father out and entreated him."

It will not be found at last that the Father's heart has

failed toward any of His creatures. How solemn is His protestation,—"*As I live*, saith the Lord, I have no pleasure in the death of him that dieth: wherefore turn yourselves, and live ye." No: men must tear themselves out of the arms which are ready to inclose them. God is not estranged from us,—needs no reconciliation, although men's creeds may impute it to Him. "We pray in Christ's stead, Be *ye* reconciled to God." (2 Cor. v. 20.) Man indeed needs his heart changed. Listen to the elder son, and you will find the grudge which is in the heart of many religionists: "But he said unto his father, 'Lo, these many years do I serve thee, neither transgressed I at any time thy commandments; and yet thou never gavest me a kid, that I might make merry with my friends. But as soon as this thy son is come, who hath devoured thy living with harlots, thou has killed for him the fatted calf.'"

Thus it is plain, men may be busy for God, with all along a grudge in the heart against God. Their blank and cheerless lives, spite of all that they can do, witness against them; but they would fling the accusation against God. Their hearts are not with Him. They have "friends" to whom they turn to find what with Him they cannot. They take outwardly His yoke, but they do not find it easy: there is no fulfillment of that—"Ye shall find rest to your souls."

Who is in fault? How vain to think that God is! How impossible to find aught but perfection in the Holy One! Do that, and indeed you will stop all the harps of heaven, darken its blessed light, and bring in disaster and ruin everywhere. There is no fear: He will be justified in His sayings, and overcome when He is judged. But it is an old contention, and a frequent one: "Wilt thou also disannul my judgment? wilt thou condemn me that thou mayest be righteous?" Ah, we must do that, or submit to that judgment of God ourselves; for it is recorded as to us, "There is none righteous,—no, not one," and "what things soever the law saith, it saith to them that are under the law, that every mouth may be stopped, and all the world become guilty before God."

To take this place is repentance, and then we are Pharisees no longer. We *need* grace, and thus we come to understand it. We understand it, and so appreciate it. We find it in God, and thus turn to Him. How sweet is then His voice! and how the spring of joy begins to bubble up within the soul! Repentance and faith are never separate, and the tear of penitence is the dew of the Spirit, that already sparkles in the morning brightness —fuller of joy itself than all the pleasures of sin can make one for a moment!

Of this the elder son knows nothing. His heart is shut up in self-righteousness, and there is nothing that can harden a heart more. Self-righteousness claims its due, and sees nothing but its due in all the blessing God can shower upon it. The more it gets, the more it values itself upon it. The getting so much is proof positive of so much merit. Poverty and misfortune (as the world calls it) are equal proofs of demerit, except indeed when they come upon itself, and then they are unrighteousness in God. So the heart is, as the Scripture expresses it, "shut up in its own fat," insensible, even to the grossest stupidity, or living but to murmur out its folly and its shame.

But the father's words seem to many to refute this account of the elder son. How could he say to such an one as this, "Son, thou art ever with me, and all that I have is thine"? Does God speak to the self-righteous and unsaved after this manner? Could it be said of them that they are ever with God, or that all that He has is theirs? If so, would it not seem as if after all they had the better portion?

We have only to look, however, at the facts of the parable to find a convincing answer to all this. Let us take these two things separately, and inquire what is the real truth as to each.

First, "Thou art ever with me." This must of course express a fact, but what is the fact? That the elder son was with the father, had lived a decorous life, and not wandered as the younger had, is plain upon the surface; and it is not strange that the father should express his approbation of that. The open sins of publican and harlot certainly are not, in God's eyes, better, or as good, as the moral and well-ordered life of the respectable religionist. So the woman in Simon's house the Lord evidently puts down as owing the five hundred pence, rather than the fifty; and of her He says, "Her sins, *which are many*, are forgiven." It would not magnify God's grace to say that because they were minor sinners it flowed forth so freely to "publicans and harlots," nor is there ever any such reason given. He does not set a premium upon vice—God forbid!—but all natural laws, and all His government among men operate against it. Even the infidel, as to Scripture, allows in nature a "power that makes for righteousness"—meaning by that too just what the Pharisee would mean. Thus the father's, "Son, thou art ever with me," has its basis of truth.

To make out the complete meaning, however, we must certainly supplement it with something else than this. That there was inward nearness to the father upon the son's part is impossible to believe: he had never rewarded his toil with even a kid for festivity with his friends! And in truth the Father makes no provision for merriment elsewhere, and would have no "friends" recognized outside His household.

There was no real nearness to the father, then, in this elder son, and we cannot supplement thus the thought of his outward nearness. What remains for us? Surely as to the younger, so to the elder, it was the father's *heart* that spoke; and from *his* side, "Thou art ever near me," tells of One who is not distant from His creatures, in whose heart they dwell near indeed. Yes, He is not far from every one of us; and of this He would persuade the Pharisee no less than the prodigal. "God so loved the *world*, that He gave His only begotten Son, that whosoever believeth on Him should not perish, but have everlasting life."

But "all that I have is thine"? That is plainly an earthly portion, not a heavenly. If we look at the beginning of the parable, we find that the father had divided between his two sons his living. The younger had spent his portion, wasted it with harlots,—plainly the earthly things, which God does entirely divide to His offspring by creation. To the elder, there still belonged his: he had not squandered it, and it was all that was left. Heavenly grace, when it bestows the best robe, does not thereby give back the lost health, the wasted substance, the natural things which may be gone forever. These things belong still to the prudent and careful liver, such as the elder son was. The meaning here should be very plain, and God would thus appeal to those who, receiving daily from His hand, are yet content to live in practical distance from Him. "The goodness of God leadeth to repentance."

But He keeps to His grace: "It was meet that we should make merry and be glad; for this thy brother was dead, and is alive again; and was lost, and is found."

# THE PERSEVERANCE OF THE SAINTS.

THE question as to what is commonly called "the perseverance of the saints," includes in it another and a most serious one. That question is as to the footing upon which the believer, justified by faith, stands before God. Thus it is a point of the greatest moment to ascertain what the Scripture truth is. It is not too much to say, that the nature and character of the peace which as Christians we enjoy, and of our life and walk as such, are all materially affected by the view we entertain with regard to the truth before us.

I would at once then put the question, What is the nature of the salvation we have received, and what the footing upon which we now stand as believers before God?

1. Clearly, we stand as such, before God "in Christ," "accepted in the Beloved." (Eph. i. 6.) Christ in glory, risen from the dead, having finished in our behalf the work of atonement, stands as our representative in the presence of God. So fully, that what He has passed through for us *we* are accredited with. Thus we are said to be "dead," "buried," "quickened," and "raised up" *with Him;* and even "seated together in heavenly places *in Christ* Jesus." (Rom. vi. 8; Eph. ii. 5, 6.) His being in heaven for us is thus as if we had actually gone in there and taken possession already of our final home; and there we are, presented to the eye and heart of God

as identified with Him who, "when He had by Himself purged our sins, sat down at the right hand of the Majesty on high."

Our former state and condition as sinners has thus found its judgment in the cross. "Our old man was crucified with Christ:"—not *should*, or *shall* be, but "was;" not was crucified *in me*, but "*with Him*." (Rom. vi.) Thus, for God and for faith, the old standing has passed away. "We are not in the flesh"(Rom. viii. 9); "not of the world, even as Christ is not of the world." (John xvii. 14.) To sum up all in a word, the apostle's words as to the Christian's place are, "If any man be in Christ, he is a new creature: old things are passed away; behold, *all* things are become new." (2 Cor. v. 17.)

I know that all these things are read, or sought to be read, in the light of experience, and referred to an inward work in the soul instead of to our place in Christ, and what belongs to it. Yet Scripture says distinctly in this last case, as in others, "if any man be *in Christ*," and then uses expressions which would certainly not be true of "*any* man in Christ," (mark) if applied to the inward work. "*All* things new," who indeed can pretend to, that knows anything of himself? Thus these blessed texts taken from their true application are made instruments of self-torture for souls seeking honestly but blindly to find in themselves evidences that they are accepted of God. While, with the eye on Christ, and the knowledge that we are in Him, and therefore, "as He is, so are we" (1 John iv. 17), they become the sweetest, fullest assurances of where divine love has placed us, and what we are to God as in His Son. Is there any "old thing" in Him? If I am thus accepted of God, are not the "old things passed away"? are not "all things become new"? Yes, indeed, wholly. I can take it in the simplest way,

## THE PERSEVERANCE OF THE SAINTS. 143

and believe it to the fullest extent, and find it unutterable joy, and only that.

Well, this is how we are accepted. We have travelled through death in Christ, and come up out of it. We have taken possession, in Him, already of our place above. We are accepted of Him where no whit of the "old things" is found. Look at this, beloved reader, and then answer me, oh answer me—is this *security?* Will Christ fail to satisfy God? Will God, who has accepted Him for me, repent, and again turn to what I am? Alas for me if He does! Alas for me and for you; and that, not at our worst, but at our best!

But no; that is impossible; for with Christ—in Christ's death—we have died. "He that is dead is justified from sin." (Rom. vi. 7, *margin.*) Our life, our history, ended with the cross in complete and utter judgment. We live before God in Christ alone. His own words are now, "Because *I* live, ye shall live also." (John xiv. 19.)

2. And thus have we "peace;" and upon such ground as this is "peace" in the proper sense alone possible. I need scarcely waste words in proving that it is peace that God is preaching by Jesus Christ (Acts x. 36); and that, "being justified by faith, we have *peace* with God through our Lord Jesus Christ." (Rom. x. 1.) Not only "the full assurance of faith" (Heb. x. 22), but "the full assurance of *hope*" also is what God designs for us. (Heb. vi. 11.) This is peace as to the past, the present, *and the future;* and this is alone true peace. However blessed my portion in the present, if there is danger that I lose it, who shall say I ought not to be afraid? It is no comfort to say to me, "It all depends upon yourself," when "myself" is just what I have learned most of all to be afraid of. Ought I to have "perfect peace" in looking onward to the future, if it is to consist in assurance that *I* shall never backslide

J

and depart, though many have! If I read, "Thou wilt keep him in perfect peace, whose mind is stayed on Thee," I can understand that, if I may trust Him for the future too. If I may say, in confidence that I have committed my soul into His hands, "I know whom I have believed, and am persuaded that He is able to *keep* what I have committed unto Him against that day" (2 Tim. i. 12), then indeed all is well. If He will not keep it, except I do my part (little or much), then how can it be peace?

To trust Him fully, if He be all in it, is surely well, and what I ought to do; but, on the other hand, I *ought* to *dis*trust myself. "Let him that thinketh he standeth, take heed lest he fall." But if I am not to think I stand, and yet my salvation depends upon my standing, ought I to be at rest?

3. But, blessed be God, it is not so. Perfected as a Saviour through the suffering of the cross, Christ is become "the author of *eternal* salvation unto all them that obey Him." (Heb. v. 9.) What is "eternal" salvation? and when do I receive it? Well, Paul says to us, that God "HATH saved us." (2 Tim. i. 9.) Is not that, then, "eternal salvation"? If *I* have obeyed Him—for the gospel calls for obedience, most surely (Rom. x. 16)—if I have obeyed His call of grace, and come to Him, is He not the author of eternal salvation to me just then? or must I wait till there is no more danger before I can speak of being saved for ever?

4. But redemption, too, is eternal. "He hath entered in once into the holy place, having obtained *eternal redemption* for us. (Heb. ix. 12.) Well, are we redeemed? Yes, assuredly, "we HAVE *redemption* through His blood, the forgiveness of sins, according to the riches of His grace. (Eph. i. 7.) Is that, then, "for ever"? Alas!

through how many of the plainest testimonies of Scripture the legality and unbelief of the human heart will work their way. Yet there it lies, the only true and perfect rest for the conscience, as we are witness to ourselves; there it lies before us, preaching peace without presumption, because "peace through Jesus Christ." Will He rebuke me, think you, because I cast this burden with all other burdens on Himself? May I not cast this care for the future too upon Him? Will He not justify my trust? Will He not care also for this?

5. But my "life," too, is "eternal." I already *have* "everlasting life." How He has compassed me about with these eternities, as if to build me up an infinite rampart against doubt! For thus saith the Lord Himself, "Verily, verily, I say unto you, He that heareth my word and believeth on Him that sent me, HATH everlasting life, and shall *not* come into condemnation; but is passed from death unto life." (John v. 24.)

Beloved reader, these are the Lord's own words. Solemnly uttered and affirmed as truth, they link the present and the future of the believer indissolubly together. He says, the one who *has* eternal life (in the present) *shall* not (in the future) come into condemnation. Do you believe that? There is no "guarding" of that statement, such as men suggest; no "if" nor "but" to mar the blessed peace that that assurance gives. Are you going to put it in? Are you going to bring some other Scripture to qualify or modify the simple meaning of this? It is in vain; for "Scripture cannot be broken," and He who gave it cannot so deny Himself. The whole idea of balancing one passage with another, as if, taken simply as they stand, they were opposed to one another, is false, and a fatal denial of the truth of God. What simple soul could lay hold of the truth in a statement which had to be balanced with an unknown number of other statements, before the precise meaning could be settled? The divine Lover of men's souls could not speak so to them. He could not use words which, taken simply and literally as they stand, would deceive. No, He could not do this. And thus, if I get what really He has said, I may be sure He has said nothing else to contradict or empty it of meaning. I may rest my soul upon it safely. I may build on it as on a rock.

I know few sadder signs of the little authority the word of God has in the present day, than this deplorable habit of ranging Scripture against Scripture. On one side a text is produced; instead of reverent inquiry as to what it means, a text in opposition to it, as men deem, is produced. James' "justification by works" is put in the one scale; Paul's "justification by faith" in the other. Arminian texts are balanced with Calvinistic. Alas! God's word is gone as an authority, and common sense and human reason become supreme judges as to the side on which the scale of truth inclines.

How unlike our Lord's "Verily, verily!" What a relief to come back to that out of the fog of human uncertainty! "He spake as One that had authority, and not as the scribes." Do you fear to trust Him, beloved reader, apart from all His commentators? Certainly, then, what He says of the believer is, that he *has* everlasting life, and *shall* not come into condemnation, but—here is the confirmation of it—*is* passed from death unto life. His future condition is settled by his present one; for already he *has* "EVERLASTING life." He is alive to God for ever.

6. The Lord repeats this in another well-known passage: "My sheep hear my voice, and I know them, and they follow me: and I give unto them eternal life; and

they shall never perish, neither shall any one pluck them out of my hand." (John x. 27, 28.)

Now, if anything could add strength to the former statement, it would be precisely what we find here. For it is not only now, "I give them eternal life, and they shall never perish;" but if people suggest, "It is only if they hear Christ's word," "it is only while they follow Him," this is met by the assertion, My sheep *do* hear my voice;" "they *do* follow me." You may say, if you will, "not always," "not continually;" but our Lord says nothing one way or other about that. He takes for granted, so to speak, that they do hear and follow. You have no right to suppose anything else. It is not said that they hear always, or follow without any straying; still on the whole they hear and follow, and He gives them eternal life, and they *never* perish, nor shall any pluck them out of His hand. If you say (with some) they may pluck themselves out, *then* they would perish; but, He says, they never shall.

7. One more text on this side of the question, and as to this point more decisive perhaps for many. The apostle John, with the case of certain apostates before him, tells us in words that apply to very many since: "They went out from us, but they were not of us; for if they *had been* of us, they would no doubt have *continued* with us: but they went out, that they might be made manifest that they were not all of us." (1 John ii. 19.)

The decisiveness of this passage in connection with those just quoted, is in its taking up so simply and decidedly just the point which many think to be uncovered by the others. It asserts without any qualification the exact doctrine of the "perseverance of the saints:"—"if they had been of us, they *would* have continued with

148       THE PERSEVERANCE OF THE SAINTS.

us;" their going out made it manifest that they were not of us.*

Surely than this nothing can be plainer or more complete. With this, then, we may end the direct proofs of the doctrine. We have found the foundation of it to be a standing in Christ before God, which cannot change because He cannot. We have found that as sinners we had our death and judgment in the cross of Christ, and are now in Him, the old things passed away entirely. We have found that God has saved us, and that salvation is eternal; that we have also "eternal redemption" and "everlasting life;" that the Lord's own assertion as to His own is, that they shall not come into condemnation, nor ever perish; that His sheep do hear His voice, and follow Him; and that the apostle tells us that *real* Christians *will* "continue" such.

I beseech, again, my reader's earnest attention to the point, that thus, too, alone is perfect peace with God possible—peace as to the past, the present, and the future—"*full* assurance of hope" without presumption.

The way is now open to look at the passages, which are supposed to teach the possibility of salvation being lost.

A large number—I might say, the largest number by far—of the texts which seem to imply the possibility of the soul being lost that has once believed unto salvation, belong to a class of which 1 Cor. ix. 27 furnishes the most striking example. It is thus the passage most frequently of all upon the lips of objectors. They ask commonly,

---

\* The force of the original is, "that none were of us," which the whole passage proves to be the only possible sense. "All are not" is a Greek idiom for "none are," as in Matt. xxiv. 22 : "*no* flesh should be saved," which is literally, "all flesh should not be saved;" or in Luke i. 37 : "with God everything shall not be impossible," *i.e.* "nothing shall be impossible."

the moment you speak of being safe for ever, "Was not Paul himself afraid of being a castaway?" But the text says nothing about any *fear* he had. It does say this, "I keep under my body, and bring it into subjection: lest that by any means, when I have preached to others, I myself should be a castaway."

It would be poor work to seek in anywise to blunt or evade the force of such Scriptures. They have their use most surely in the divine wisdom which inspired them. But just precisely because they have, we must enquire the more carefully what exactly they *do* mean. The word of God will bear the strictest and most thorough examination. Precise accuracy will only be shunned by those who either on the one hand have little faith in the perfect inspiration of every word of it, or else fear to face honestly the full light of truth.

Now it is remarkable, upon looking at such passages as that before us, that they none of them put things in the way which would be simplest and easiest to put them, supposing eternal life or salvation were things that might be lost. They do *not* say, "lest, after I have been saved, I myself should be a castaway," or "lest, after being born again," or "lest, after having had eternal life, I myself should be a castaway." Such passages are not to be found anywhere in Scripture, and surely that is to be marked. How easy for divine wisdom to have settled the whole question for any honest believer by a single sentence of that sort! But there is nothing of the kind. The supposition in the text is, that one who had "*preached to others*" might *himself* "be a castaway." But who doubts that? And who doubts, or ought to doubt, that, as there is a way of holiness, which leads to everlasting life, on the one hand, so there is on the other a way of sin, of *un*holiness, of license to the lusts of the flesh, which if a man takes, will lead him to eternal death?

If we were to question this, we should have to deny some of the plainest passages of Scripture. Take 1 Cor. vi. 9, 10, for example: what can be plainer? "Know ye not that the unrighteous shall *not* inherit the kingdom of God? *Be not deceived*," and this, mark, is addressed to professing Christians, "neither fornicators, nor idolaters, nor adulterers," and so on, "shall inherit the kingdom of God."

This is most plain and most weighty. It makes it quite plain that the gospel is not intended to be an allowance of sin, but salvation *from* it. Where really received, it brings a man *out* of the things it finds him in, and sets him in the way of holiness. As the apostle goes on here: "And such *were* some of you; but ye are washed, but ye are sanctified," etc. And again, as in Titus ii. 11, 12, "the grace of God that bringeth salvation hath appeared, . . . teaching us that, denying ungodliness and worldly lusts, we should live soberly, righteously, and godly, in this present world." The grace which saves makes holy.

This is not limiting the freeness of the gospel, nor diminishing its fulness. It is only the maintaining its real character and power. It is not that we are brought under legal conditions. It is not that we are told, that we shall be saved if we walk aright; but that God has saved us, that we *may* walk right. In the words of Eph. ii. 10., "we," believers, "are His workmanship, created in Christ Jesus unto good works, which God hath before ordained (or, as in the margin, prepared) that we should walk in them."

Thus God has linked together in the simplest and most decisive way, without in the least weakening or modifying the previous assurance of His grace in the gospel, "good works" with salvation. Put in this way, that those created anew in Christ are at the same time created unto them. If then the loudest profession of faith in Christ be associated with an ungodly walk, Scripture teaches me how to form my judgment of that profession. It tells me, that "as many as are led by the Spirit of God, *they* are the sons of God." (Rom. viii. 14.) It teaches me that I am not to dishonor the precious gospel of grace by allowing that it has taken effect in the salvation of a soul, where it has not at the same time changed the heart and life.

Now this is precisely one important use of such passages as that we are considering. He who saw, even while these epistles were being written, the evil at work —and who *fore*saw the immense mass of false profession which has since come in—has left these words, and such as these, on record, to test the reality of it all, and that He might not be dishonored by the ungodly lives of mere professors being taken as what His gospel might, if not *produce*, at least permit. "Faith, if it have not works, is dead, being alone" (James ii. 17); so does the word of God fully teach. We must not put down others, nor must we expect to be put down *by* others, as true believers, truly saved ones, except as the power of that grace which saves is seen in its purifying influence upon the walk and life.

Thus there is a way which leads to life, and a way of death. No matter what your creed, "to whom ye yield yourselves servants to obey, *his servants ye are* to whom ye obey; whether of sin unto death, or of obedience unto righteousness." (Rom. vi. 16.)

This is the key to the language of the apostle in 1 Cor. ix. 27. Addressing, as he does, "all that call on the name of Jesus Christ our Lord," whether at Corinth or elsewhere (ch. i. 2), he tells them for himself that he was one who was upon this way of life. He kept under his body, and brought it into subjection, not tolerating its lusts, nor walking in fleshly indulgence, in order not to be a "castaway;" *i. e.* one rejected or reprobate. He had no fear of being such. He took the way which led him heavenward joyfully and confidently, "not uncertainly." He knew the grace which had called him with a holy calling would not fail to carry him through. He knew that God had saved him already, and given him, *not* the spirit of fear, but of power, and of love, and of a sound mind. (2 Tim. i. 7–9.) And he yielded himself up intelligently and joyfully, to be led along the way of holiness unto "the end, everlasting life." If any, professing faith in Christ, were doing otherwise, he meant to warn them by his example what faith did for the soul who had it; because only "as many as are led by the Spirit of God, they are the sons of God."

This in nowise implies that those who are sons of God may cease to be so by refusing to be led of the Spirit. That is mere human argument, and of the poorest kind; for not only do plain Scriptures, as we have seen, forbid the supposition, but it is in real opposition to the passage itself; for (it tells us) the sons of God are those who *are* led. And there is nothing said in the whole context to show that continuance is at all in question. Those who are sons are simply marked out from those that are not.

It is quite true, too, that true children of God may, alas! be dull and careless, and poor followers of such a leader. They may fall and get bemired with the slough of sin. I dare not say what a believer might not do, if not cleaving closely to his Guide and Strength. What David did, what Peter did, are solemn warnings for all time. Still one easily discerns that these were things the result of sloth and self-confidence, fallen into, not sought out, and from which He who had them in His care recovered them. *Characteristically*, even of a David or a Peter, surely we could say, they were led of the Spirit of God, and manifested to be His sons. At a particular moment, they might not manifest what they were. But it is only of what is characteristic this text in Romans speaks. It is the determining for us where the line is to be drawn between those born of God in reality and those only assuming to be so; a rule we may not in many instances be able to apply, but which has none the less immense value, because it frees the gospel (as I have already said) from that charge of giving license to sin, which men are always ready and eager to bring against it.

How many would object to us in that way, their own supposition (which they have no title to make) of believers falling into open sin, and going on, and dying in it; and then turn round on us with the question, Would such an one be saved? To all that the one sufficient answer is, "As many as are led by the Spirit of God, they are the sons of God." You have no right therefore to make the supposition; the latter part of what you suppose would (for me) make entirely untrustworthy the claim to *be* a believer.

These passages, then, are guards against the "turning the grace of God into lasciviousness," a thing which Jude notices as done in his day (*v*. 4), and which certainly there is no less danger of in the present. On the other hand, legality is never a real guard of holiness, but the destruction of it. "The strength of sin is the law;" and to put the fear of falling away before a soul, in order to keep him right, is only to pervert the whole character of his life and service. Just so far as he takes up the motive we present to him, he becomes really one living to himself, in a religious way no doubt; but none the less really, and none the less offensively to God. The love of Christ, it is assumed, will not keep me straight, except a large measure of self-love works along with it! What a dishonor to Him, and what a lowering of the whole character of God's work in the soul of a saint! Except I am in danger of eternal damnation, I shall be sure to go wrong. But the Lord says, "If ye love Me, keep my commandments;" and the apostle, "Though I give my body to be burned, and have not love" ("charity" in the common version), "it profiteth me nothing" (1 Cor. xiii. 3); the apostle John again, "There is *no fear* in love." (1 John iv. 18.) How does all this agree with the advocacy of a principle essentially and necessarily a principle of fear? for if there is danger of being lost, I ought certainly to be afraid of it.

There are some other texts, nearly akin to the standard passage in Corinthians, which we may now take up. I believe we shall find, if we have got hold of what has now been before us, that we have already the key to the understanding of these also. In Col. i. 22, 23, for example: "To present you holy and unblameable and unreproveable in His sight: *if* ye continue in the faith grounded and settled, and be not moved away from the hope of the gospel;" or again, in Heb. iii. 6: "Whose house are we, *if* we hold fast the confidence and the rejoicing of the hope firm unto the end;" and verse 14: "For we are made partakers of Christ, *if* we hold the beginning of our confidence stedfast unto the end." Addressing a number of professed Christians, these "ifs" had their right and necessary place. Men *were* giving up faith in Christ, as this epistle to the Hebrews conclusively shows. The warning was perfectly in place. Nor could men be saved while giving up this faith; drawing back from Christ would be drawing back unto perdition. Yet this same apostle could in the selfsame epistle put those who had believed unto salvation in a different class altogether from those who could so apostatize: "*We* are not of them who draw back unto perdition"—not simply, "who *have* drawn back," which there could be no need to say, but "who draw back;" we are not the sort of people who do that —"but of them that believe to the saving of the soul;" that is the class to which we belong, and it is a different one to the other.

Most clearly, then, the apostle did not mean that *such* believers, positively saved ones, could draw back unto perdition. It was needful, on the other hand, to warn professors about it for two reasons at least. First, because the giving up of Christ put outside the possibility of salvation altogether, for none else could save. Secondly, because it was and is important, that men should not rest in a faith they had, or thought they had, in times past, which was not true for the present moment. Faith that I had faith once is not faith in Christ, and may be a dream of my own. Just so, the vain argument that "I *was* converted once, and therefore"—which is vain because it is a mere belief in what my heart may have deceived me. If I am trusting my conversion or my faith, the result may prove I had neither. If I trust *Christ, He* cannot deceive, and so I am safe. "Blessed are *all* they that put their trust in *Him.*" (Ps. ii. 12.)

There was need to guard a point like that, to prevent men putting "I trusted" for "I trust." "I trusted," is my own thought of what I did. "I trust," makes Christ indeed the object of that trust. Therefore it was needful to say your confidence must be a thing held fast, if you are to be presented blameless in His sight at last.

Belief there might have been, of a certain sort, in Christ, without its being to salvation. Such faith, never having been of divine workmanship, had a natural tendency to wear out and come to nothing. We see many instances in every one of the (so-called) "revival" movements. Nor are they a proof necessarily of anything wrong in the preaching which produces them. The Lord gives us in Matthew xiii. plain assurance that where the true seed of the gospel is sown, and He the Sower of it, such things will occur. There will be cases such as his who "heareth the word, and anon (immediately) with joy receiveth it; yet hath he not root in himself, but *dureth for a while*: for when tribulation or persecution ariseth because of the Word, by-and-by he is offended." Such a man believes: he is not insincere, not a hypocrite; simply, the Word, like seed in stony ground, has no *root* in him; his heart, never ploughed up by conviction of sin, remains in unchanged hardness. The joy in him was too "immediate;" there was no finding out of self, no taking the place of lost, that Christ might save. He believed a doctrine; never came to Jesus. He had joy, not peace. There was no change in the man himself, and no root. Mark, it was not what had root that withered, but because it had *no* root it withered away. It would not have withered had it had root.

Scripture then, which teaches that there is such a thing as "believing for a while," teaches too its character. And while we see the need of the admonition as to the necessity of continuance in the faith, we see also abundantly that those who believe to the saving of the soul belong at all times to a different class from those who draw back unto perdition.

There are yet some passages, however, which require special notice. Thus undoubtedly Heb. vi. 4–8 furnishes us with the example of hopeless apostacy; and the previous condition of these apostates is described in terms which appear to many altogether too strong to apply to unconverted professors merely. They "were once enlightened," had "tasted of the heavenly gift," and been "made partakers of the Holy Ghost," had "tasted the good word of God, and the powers of the world to come." It is just this which makes their case so hopeless, that all the goodness of God, as displayed in Christianity, has been, so to speak, spent in vain upon them. Or rather, it has been as rain from heaven nurturing only thorns and briers in the unfruitful soil. Yet, the apostle adds, as to those in whom he *had* seen fruit (*v.* 10), "beloved, we are persuaded better things of you, and things which accompany salvation, though we thus speak." (*v.* 9.) Thus, again he carefully guards himself from being misunderstood to mean that those whose faith had works, and had thus proved itself a living faith, could so fall away.

This alone, for really simple souls, might suffice as to the whole passage. It surely ought to be enough to hear the apostle say that, although he is speaking thus, he is persuaded better things of those who have shown "work and labor of love toward His name." Yet it is well to enquire, in its place, from what the men before us here apostatize. But observe again, then, there is no mention of their having been born again, or converted, or justified, or saved, or having had forgiveness of sins, or eternal life. Of none who are declared to be in that condition is there ever any doubt of their security, or any hint that after all they might be lost. On the contrary, the thought is carefully guarded against, as we have seen.

But as to these—

They were "enlightened." And "the true light *lighteth* every man which cometh into the world" (John i. 9); but that this is not necessarily saving knowledge is plain. There may be conviction where there is no conversion, as every day shows. Yet how perilous to turn from the light which has thus borne witness to our souls!

They had "tasted of the heavenly gift," and "of the good word of God." But so had he who received seed upon the stony ground; he "immediately *with joy* received it." We see that too, often. The word is welcomed; it is not *understood*. Only "he who received seed into the *good* ground is he that heareth the Word, and *understandeth it*." (Matt. xiii. 23.) It is possible thus to have a false peace patched up, and to find joy in a gospel, which after all has never been apprehended by the soul, and has never brought forth fruit in it at all.

Besides this, they "were made partakers of the Holy Ghost," and had tasted of "the powers of the world to come." This last expression refers to miraculous powers,* and the "world to come" is literally the "coming age." Here, as elsewhere, it refers to the millennium, when the signs and wonders which signalized the early days of Christianity will be repeated. The prophet Joel (ii. 28, 29) witnesses of this; and his prophecy the apostle Peter could take up at Pentecost, and apply to what God did by His Spirit at that time. Yet the prophesy itself, however much it might take in Pentecost, goes on to the restoration of Israel in the last days. Miracles could therefore fitly be called "powers of the coming age." But we have the Lord's assurance that men might *thus* be "partakers of the Holy Ghost"—prophesy and do mir-

---

\* The word (dunameis) in the plural is only used either for "miracles" (as chap. ii. 4, for instance), or for angelic orders, "principalities and *powers*," or once in the expression (Matt. xxiv. 29; Mark xiii. 25; Luke xxi. 26): "the *powers* of the heavens shall be shaken."

acles (which could be done only through the Holy Ghost) —and yet after all He might say to them, "I *never* knew you." (Matt. vii. 22, 23.) It is clear therefore that in this sense they might be "partakers of the Holy Ghost" and yet be lost. The Spirit crying "Abba, Father," in us is another thing. Those who are thus "sealed by that Holy Spirit of promise" are "sealed unto the day of redemption." (Eph. i. 13; iv. 30.) In this case therefore there is no possibility of being lost.

We see, then, that what we are assured by the constant tenor of the word of God, and by the very context of the passage itself, *must* have been the condition of those who are spoken of as drawing back unto perdition, is confirmed by the very terms by which they are described. For none of these imply that they were either born again or justified. They had now openly given up Christ, and by going back to the ranks of those who had crucified Him, "crucified to themselves the Son of God afresh, and put Him to an open shame." It is open apostacy that is in question, going back to the Judaism out of which they had come, and what hope could there be for such?

The "wilful sin" of chap. x. 26 is plainly of the same nature. People were forsaking the Christian assembly (v. 25), taking the place of "adversaries" to Christ (v. 27), treading under foot the Son of God, counting the blood of the covenant by which they had been "sanctified" (or set apart as Christians) an unholy thing. They might say perhaps, "Well, after all, we have God's own appointed sacrifices still." But the apostle answers, that upon that ground "there remaineth *no more* sacrifice for sins," nothing that has virtue to cleanse a sinner ; but, on the contrary, "a certain fearful looking-for of judgment and of fiery indignation which shall devour the adversaries."

There may be those who read this who may be otherwise troubled at these verses, and I cannot refrain from adding a word for such. Many do not see that the hopelessness of the state of those described consists in this, that they have given up the only ground upon which salvation is possible. It is not mere failure, getting into the world or into sin, that these verses speak of. It is the wilful rejection of Christ as Saviour. They crucify Him afresh, trample Him under foot, count the blood of the covenant an unholy thing. In a word, it is not any mere ordinary backsliding, as I have said, but apostacy from Christianity itself, and that is hopeless.

Beside this, there is another thing. The "impossibility" spoken of in Heb. vi. is impossibility to renew them again unto *repentance*. There was no impossibility in their being saved, if they *did* repent. The word remains ever true for all, while this day of gospel grace lasts—"Whosoever will, let him take the water of life freely." If any one *will*, therefore, he may. No sin is unpardonable to such, or can shut him out from the salvation that is in Christ Jesus.

But I pass on to the consideration of another example of apostacy which is given in 2 Peter ii. 20, 22: "For if after they have escaped the pollutions of the world through the knowledge of the Lord and Saviour Jesus Christ, they are again entangled therein and overcome, the latter end is worse with them than the beginning. . . . . But it is happened unto them according to the true proverb, The dog is turned to his own vomit again; and the sow that was washed, to her wallowing in the mire."

Now here again there is said to have been "the knowledge of the Lord and Saviour Jesus Christ" in those who, without doubt, "draw back unto perdition." And not only so, but this knowledge had had effect upon them, for it had drawn them out of "the pollutions of the world."

Yet it does not require any very close attention to the apostle's words, to discern here also how little he conceived these apostates to have ever been true Christians. Why had it passed into a proverb that the dog would return to his vomit again, and the washed sow to her wallowing in the mire? What did such a proverb mean, but that a washed sow *remained all the while* a sow, and that, inasmuch as the washing had not changed her nature, she would go back as a matter of course to her old habits? It was simple enough to know she would. And so one who had in the same way been merely washed from the *pollutions* of the world—from defilements from without—but whose nature was never changed, might be expected to fulfil that proverb.

But now mark the difference, as pointed out in this same epistle, where there was true faith. Speaking of those to whom that knowledge of God and of Jesus our Lord was indeed eternal life, he describes them as "having escaped," not the pollutions merely, but "the *corruption* that is in the world through lust." (Chap. i. 4.) Here the need of the soul had indeed been divinely met. It is not in this case external pollution merely, but the "lust," the internal corruption of the heart, that is dealt with. Christ is known as the rest and satisfaction of the soul. The heart is changed; with a *new* nature, new desires, new affections have come in; and there is no proverb, that if a sow be turned into a sheep it will go back into the mire.

Thus, then, we have looked at the most prominent of the texts, which might seem to imply the possibility of the soul being finally lost that has once believed unto salvation. It is not likely that other passages will present much difficulty, if the truth as to these is once distinctly seen. There is but one other text which I would briefly, in closing, remark upon; first, because it furnishes the very expression, "falling from grace," which is the technical one with many for their whole doctrine; and secondly, because there is not a passage which more distinctly marks the deeply important principle which is in question. The words in full are these:

"Christ is become of none effect unto you, whosoever of you *are justified by the* LAW; YE are fallen from *grace*." (Gal. v. 4.)

The mere quotation of the passage ought to be enough, one would think, to expose the common misapplication of it. It is he who goes back from the grace of the Gospel to justify himself by the deeds of the law—it is this man, the legalist, and not the one fallen into immorality, or gone back into the world, who is "fallen from grace." And the meaning is not that even to such God ceases to be gracious, but that the *man* has left that ground himself.

Now it is just the principle contained in this that is so important. What is it to be "justified by the law"? Does he who maintains that "man must do his part and God will do His" approach or not that ground of being justified by the law? Law works are not bad works. "Thou shalt love the Lord thy God" is its first and great commandment; and the second is like unto it—"Thou shalt love thy neighbor as thyself." Thus the law is holy; and the commandment holy, and just, and good. Yet "as many as are *of* the works of the law"—standing upon that ground before God—"are under the curse." Where then are they who suppose that *their* love to God or man, their maintenance of good works, will have something at least to do with their final salvation? Doubtless with many the language of their heart is beyond that of their creed. And there we must leave it.

Let us close with the confident assurance of the apostle's words—the words of the Holy Ghost by him:

"God commendeth His love toward us, in that, while we were *yet* sinners, Christ died for us. MUCH MORE THEN, being *now* justified by His blood, we *shall* be saved from wrath through Him. For if, when we were enemies, we were reconciled to God by the death of His Son, MUCH MORE, *being* reconciled, we *shall* be saved by His life." (Rom. v. 8–10.)

Christian reader, is that *your* assurance?

F. W. G.

www.ingramcontent.com/pod-product-compliance
Lightning Source LLC
Chambersburg PA
CBHW071433160426
43195CB00013B/1885